ALL THE WAY

ALL THE WAY

Thine ears shall hear a word behind thee, saying,
This is the way, walk ye in it, when ye turn to
the right hand, and when ye turn to the left.

MILTON SIMON

The Bookmark
Santa Clarita, California

Library of Congress Control Number: 2003103947

Simon, Milton.
All the way / by Milton Simon.
P. cm.
ISBN 0-930227-46-8

    1. Christian Science. I. Title.

  BX6915.S56 2003   289.5
  QB103-200215

Published by
The Bookmark
Post Office Box 801143
Santa Clarita, California 91380

CONTENTS

INTRODUCTION

These selected articles by Milton Simon are a treasure-trove of small metaphysical gems. They were first published in the Christian Science periodicals. Two of his finest articles — "Undisturbed" and "All the Way" — were republished in booklets by the Christian Science Publishing Society, and are now included in this collection.

Mr. Simon's articles are especially helpful when the busy day does not allow us enough quiet time for study and prayer. We can turn to them when we want a simple idea that is easy to work with, or when we are looking for just the right thoughts to hold to in meeting a difficult situation, and we can often find in his articles some discerning passage that will enable us to rise above a false claim. His articles open up new insights into Christian Science that bring inspiration and healing.

Mr. Simon was a well-known practitioner and teacher in New York City. First listed in *The Christian Science Journal* in 1938, his life was dedicated to the Cause of Christian Science. His profound spiritual understanding shines through his writings as he makes the truth relevant to the human experience. The combination of his spirituality and his humanity enabled him to write articles that are timeless. Gathered together in this collection, they can now reach those today who are seeking a better understanding of Christian Science. Thus through his writing he continues to heal and bless humanity.

ALL THE WAY

The one all-inclusive God can never know frustration or inactivity. Deity, being omni-active Life, His creation cannot become stagnant, but must be rightly active. It consists of spiritual ideas, which abide in divine Mind and are forever unfolding harmoniously according to divine law. It would be impossible for God to create ideas that were deficient or capable of functioning imperfectly. The understanding that Love constantly controls and eternally provides for its ideas can be applied daily.

More than thirty-five years ago the employees of the old Boston Elevated Railway Company were on strike. Two friends of the writer, who needed to go downtown to the courthouse, started to walk in from the outskirts. On their way a chauffeur stopped his car to offer them a ride. He was not going downtown, he explained — only halfway, but would be glad to take them that distance.

The husband answered that they would be happy to accept. His wife said nothing but thought: "Love never takes anyone halfway. Love takes us all the way." Immediately she recognized this as an angel message and said, "Thank You, Father; that's all I need." While she was gratefully pondering the spiritual fact that Love's purpose is always fully accomplished, that the Father glorifies the son completely, that in any situation, whatever stems from Principle is finished by Principle, the chauffeur called out, "This is halfway, but I have time to take you all the way and would be glad to do so."

Of course her demonstration was not in being taken to the courthouse, but in discerning and accepting a spiritual truth. Ever since that time she has often used the truth, "Love takes us all the way." When a case of sickness has improved, she has realized that Love not only makes one better, but also heals completely. When error has argued that retrenchment was necessary, she has known that Love does not partially meet one's needs, but bestows on man the infinite resources of Soul. When facing tasks that seemed beyond her, she has recalled that divine intelligence never furnished the opportunity for a service without giving one the ability with which to perform it. Love supports whatever is constructive in our experience. Love never uncovers a selfish material tendency without supplying the unselfishness and spirituality which annihilate it. "Love takes us all the way."

Can anyone picture Jesus as believing in frustration? Then if we follow our Master, we shall not admit that God does things halfway. God does not give us a right desire and then fail to bring it to fruition. There is not a partially consummated or fruitless transaction in God's plan for His creation. As we read in the book of Zechariah, "The seed shall be prosperous; the vine shall give her fruit, and the ground shall give her increase, and the heavens shall give their dew; and I will cause the remnant of this people to possess all these things."

Even when mortal mind argues retrogression in an experience or aggravation of an illness, mental chemicalization, or the action of Truth in human consciousness, it is merely bringing evil to the surface to be destroyed. Love's healing is forever. God eternally maintains man in His likeness. Therefore one can never manifest what error falsely claims he once had. Again, there will be no frustration in our experience if we become a law unto ourselves and refuse to acquiesce in evil's argument that God does things part way. Let us rather accept the law of Love as the law governing us completely.

Man, God's idea, is never separated from, but abides in Mind. He is not a material personality in a discordant situation from which he needs to be extricated; his individuality is completely spiritual. Mary Baker Eddy writes, "To impersonalize scientifically the material sense of existence — rather than cling to personality — is the lesson of to-day." (*Miscellaneous Writings*). The relinquish-

2

ment of the false belief that a problem, whether sickness or frustration, is personal, and the recognition that it is an illusion in an impersonal, false sense, aids in demonstrating man's flawless spiritual individuality.

The truth necessary to solve every problem is present where the problem seems to be. This truth is already known to infinite, all-knowing Mind and to man, Mind's reflection. It cannot be hidden. Moreover, Love makes it evident to our thought and in our experience. Isaiah thus portrayed God's law of inevitable fruition: "And they shall build houses, and inhabit them; and they shall plant vineyards, and eat the fruit of them. They shall not build, and another inhabit; they shall not plant, and another eat: for as the days of a tree are the days of my people, and mine elect shall long enjoy the work of their hands." Fruition and accomplishment are not something outside the real man he needs to get. They are inherent in his being. He forever possesses them because he includes all the right ideas and attributes of God.

Failing to grasp the real man's spiritual nature and present perfection, mankind believes man is material, therefore subject to limitation and frustration. When a right purpose seems thwarted, it is wont to exclaim, "Another one of those things!" This expression implies that some uncontrollable evil influence exists and has acted against man's well-being. Error's false claim should be denied, not admitted. In so far as an experience is limiting or harmful, it is untrue, hence not going on in God's harmonious universe.

In Science there are none of "those things," nothing that has functioned or can work against man's perfection. God's law alone, the law of good, is operating, and it forever blesses man. God's will is, has been, and always will be done. In reality the answer to every prayer and the fulfillment of every right desire are in Mind. Let us say so with no mental reservation and obtain the benison always redounding to those who completely acknowledge God.

Because human experience is entirely subjective — the externalization of human thought — it can be improved as thought

3

is spiritualized. Mrs. Eddy declares in *Science and Health with Key to the Scriptures*, "You command the situation if you understand that mortal existence is a state of self-deception and not the truth of being." What appears as failure or frustration is a state of self-deception. Only as we are willing to admit this, are we in a mental position to "command the situation" and nullify mortal mind's claim to hinder any righteous endeavor.

We shall find that a demonstration in Christian Science has a two-fold significance. It increases our gratitude for God's allness and perfection, and spurs us on to greater achievements Spiritward. As Thomas Huxley wrote, "The rung of a ladder was never meant to rest upon, but only to hold a man's foot long enough to enable him to put the other somewhat higher." Problems met and mastered enable us to rise higher in our demonstration of reality. Then we prove practical God's promise: "And I have filled him with the spirit of God, in wisdom, and in understanding, and in knowledge, and in all manner of workmanship." It is the promise that we are filled "with the spirit of God . . . in all manner of workmanship" that mankind should unfailingly appropriate.

Duties will not seem burdensome if we understandingly claim the spontaneity and joy inherent in man as the blessed child of God. Stagnation will be ruled out of our affairs as we accept, despite sense testimony, the spiritual fact that progress, God's unopposable law of the unfoldment of good, is ever operative in man's experience. Indeed, one can refuse to be deluded into believing that the expression of Principle can ever fail to be secure, joyous, rightly active, or justly rewarded.

Not only in our duties, but when error suggests illness or duress, Love is present to deliver. If an individual fell over an embankment or into a deep, abandoned well, his companion would not just throw him a rope. His friend would encourage him to hang on, assuring him that he would be pulled to safety. The one in need would be made to feel that behind that rope were the strength and intelligence of his rescuer. Sometimes, during a sorrow or an illness, error may argue that there is nothing we can do. Yet we can hang onto the rope — that is, keep active in our consciousness the right idea which Love provides. It will always be our savior. Why? Because, as our Leader tells us: "God is not separate from the wisdom He bestows." (*Science and Health*)

The thoughts God gives are not partly effective, nor are they ever separated from Deity. On the contrary, they carry with them His intelligence, action, and power — in fact, everything necessary for their unfoldment and fruition. The inspiration of divine Mind makes an untoward experience or illness so unreal that we see it was never any part of man. Love not only heals, it wipes out every vestige of sickness and remembrance of sin.

If we feel that a healing is delayed, or that we are up against an apparent wall of frustration, we can rejoice to find that because of the revelation of Christian Science, God's law cannot be abrogated. Evil is forever unreal. In every situation Love is present to act quickly and conclusively, to "take us all the way."

Indeed, we have the same inspiration and conviction that enabled the Psalmist to record for humanity the complete, unassailable operation of the law of Love when he wrote, "I will cry unto God most high; unto God that performeth all things for me."

UNDISTURBED

In one of his discourses, Jesus told his disciples: "Hereafter I will not talk much with you: for the prince of this world cometh, and hath nothing in me." Nothing in the world could disturb Jesus or turn him from the contemplation of the Christ, Truth, which animated him. He was conscious of God as He is, and of his own true selfhood in the likeness of the divine. He understood God to be eternal Life, the one all-inclusive, frictionless Being.

There is nothing outside of God that could encroach upon Him. If there were any element of discord in infinite Being, Life would ultimately spend itself. To be eternal, Life must be without any element of friction. This one undisturbable Being is eternally expressed by each one of us because man is the reflection of infinite Life and perfect Mind.

Individuals, then, are wrong when they believe that they are in possession of disquieting tendencies or undesirable traits and that little can be done about it. How erroneous to accept as belonging to God's child any sense of irritation! Neither receptivity to healing nor the power to heal others resides in an irritated, disturbed mentality. But in the consciousness that is uplifted and at peace, the healing Christ, the power of God, is felt. So our goal is to understand and manifest our divine sonship through the tranquility inherent in us and thus to demonstrate our immunity to anxiety and disturbance.

If we can be disturbed by certain circumstances or the actions of someone else, then is not our peace of mind in a precarious state? Is not this an indication, too, that there is need for us to correct our own consciousness until every tendency to be annoyed is conquered? Actually, not the situation itself, but our own sense of it is all that is disquieting.

God's man is not disturbed. Then what is irritated at the actions of another? Usually it is egotism, pride, or self-will, claiming existence in one's consciousness. Or, it may be self-righteousness that is sometimes shocked at what it terms the enormity of error. When truth has been assimilated, one is governed by spiritual sense. Then error's pretense no longer deceives and upsets. Mortal mind has only its own erring concepts. When others seem to think wrongly about us, we know that they are thinking only of their own wrong concept of us. That, of course, in reality never touches, much less harms us. The one undisturbable Mind governs all in peace and harmony. This Mind, the Mind of every individual, does not misunderstand, but ever loves its own ideas. As Jeremiah expresses it: "For I know the thoughts that I think toward you, saith the Lord, thoughts of peace, and not of evil, to give you an expected end."

Confronted by an untoward incident, mortal mind is apt to exclaim, "What happened?" It accepts the distressing circumstances as taking place and attempts to assign a material cause for it. Christian Science denies its occurrence. It handles the situation, not as a personal experience, but as animal magnetism attempting to hide the inviolate good that is always present. What seems to be disturbing does not exist in reality, for God's allness cannot be invaded — it seems real only to unenlightened thought. It is rectified, or eliminated, as the need may be, by our correction of our erring sense of it with the understanding that everything that has presence or existence is good.

We should scientifically handle as impersonal and as nonexistent, the suggestion that we are erring mortals. We can see through evil's machinations to man's true selfhood, as never expressing any sort of imperfection. Indeed, we can be alert to every attempt of error to deceive and irritate. In our true being we are sensitive to good alone. *physically or mentally*

Nervousness and emotionalism — tension, grief, resentment, irritation — are suggestions of evil that would confuse and disturb. Individuals jeopardize their growth Spiritward when they contend for what they term their nature, their emotional tendencies, or their indulgences. To argue for them is to succumb to animal magnetism's attempt to retard healing. Erring emotions cannot cling to one who understands the real man. They have no power with which to fasten themselves onto one. But we have power from God to hold thought to good. The exercise of this true tenacity aids in destroying the false belief in erring emotional tendencies.

Today *materia medica* is claiming that many ailments are caused by nervous or emotional disturbances. Yet Truth destroys these tendencies as erring beliefs and also heals the discordant bodily conditions to which these agitated feelings seem to give rise. One should not accede to the erroneous supposition that it is wrong to thwart emotions. Even momentary indulgence prolongs, never ends, their suppositional existence. One does not become honest through stealing, nor can he demonstrate tranquility through irritation. The slightest irritation is without justification in Truth.

Beliefs in nervousness and upsetting emotions come from the ignorant assumption that man is separated from God. False belief claims that he is a mortal, controlled by material nerves. The fact is that man is spiritual, eternally at one with God, Love, controlled by Him alone, and that he is forever expressing Love's uninvadable harmonious control. The truth which saves from the belief in weak, tired nerves, nervous prostration, false stimulation, and agitating emotions is the inseparability of divine Mind and its perfect idea, man.

Peace of mind is a pearl of great price that is not to be forfeited under the pressure of aggressive sense testimony. Let us ask ourselves, "Is there anything worth being disturbed about?" The evil of being disturbed is not just that we have allowed ourselves to be upset, but that we have succumbed to error's attempt to hide ever-present good from us. When one is conscious of man's unity with divine Love, he is undisturbed, poised, and ever at peace. He expresses the firmness and stability of Principle. His orderly, disciplined mentality is not only stable, but also active in its adherence to good.

In writing of the Christ, which Jesus so perfectly expressed, Mary Baker Eddy says in *Science and Health*: "This Christ, or divinity of the man Jesus, was his divine nature, the godliness which animated him." The Christ is always acquainting us with our radiant, spiritual selfhood, and it reveals our indissoluble oneness, or unity, with God as ever satisfying and permanent. The recognition of this unity removes us from the influence of every upsetting suggestion and enables us to maintain an abiding consciousness of God's presence and love.

This consciousness includes nothing that can be disturbed, for it is a reflection of the undisturbable Mind, which is God. To thought so illumined, these healing words of our Leader, found in *Science and Health*, glow with new spiritual meaning: "Undisturbed amid the jarring testimony of the material senses, Science, *(and Christ)* still enthroned, is unfolding to mortals the immutable, harmonious, divine Principle — is unfolding Life and the universe, ever present and eternal."

Love
Truth
Soul
Spirit
Mind
Prin.

ALL IS MIND AND ITS IDEAS

Mary Baker Eddy perceived the allness of God, divine Mind, and the inevitable corollary that there is no matter. Before she gave her revelation of the Science of Jesus' theology to the world in *Science and Health*, she proved the correctness of this theology by healing disease and sin. Her discovery that all is Mind and its perfect ideas is logical and can be substantiated.

Let us start with the self-evident truth that five and five are ten. You cannot send it anywhere — it is already there. One cannot conceive of a time when five and five have not been or will not be ten. Therefore, the thought that five and five are ten is ever present, eternal, and indestructible. Because spiritual qualities, such as justice and goodness exist and are ever present and eternal, the Mind which created and includes these qualities must likewise be so. These self-evident truths confirm the ever-presence and eternality of Mind, God.

Mind is also good, one, and infinite. Intelligent Mind could not eternally consist of such opposites as good and evil. It would have to be one or the other. In algebra one cannot conceive of a minus twelve unless he knows what twelve is. Similarly, there would, in belief, be no evil or lie without something true about which to lie. Evil in every instance is only a negation or lie about some positive good which precedes it. Hence evil, the negative, is too late to be first or true. Consequently, good is primal, evil suppositional. Thus we see that Mind, or God, already proved to be ever present and eternal, must also be wholly good.

We admit, too, that Mind is self-existent and self-sustaining, for only Mind could evolve and sustain Mind. It conceives an unlimited idea of creation, and so must itself be infinite. Again, there can be but one Mind since that one is infinite and all-inclusive. Thus we see that there is one infinite, ever-present, eternal, wholly good, self-existent, self-sustaining Mind, or God.

Jesus asked: "Do men gather grapes of thorns, or figs of thistles?" And he answered his own question: "A good tree cannot bring forth evil fruit, neither can a corrupt tree bring forth good fruit." Like produces like — therefore Mind could not evolve matter or anything unlike itself. And since all must proceed from the primal Mind, there can be no matter. Mind is forever expressed, for Mind unexpressed would be a nonentity — no Mind. Mind, God, expresses itself in ideas and in no other way — hence, all that can possibly have existence is the one wholly good Mind and its perfect spiritual ideas. As our Leader tersely says: "The Scriptures imply that God is All-in-all. From this it follows that nothing possesses reality nor existence except the divine Mind and His ideas." (*Science and Health*)

Mrs. Eddy's teaching also logically makes clear the unreality of the whole belief in evil. The misconception that five and five are nine is never true. Being false, it never came into being. Correspondingly, fear and disease are not true because they do not proceed from intelligent, ever-present Mind, God. Only that which is spiritually mental or an intelligent idea could possibly have existence in Mind, in Truth. The only possible consciousness is the one omniscient, perfect Mind and that which reflects it. Let us be grateful that these fundamental truths can be applied to every discordant belief.

The assurance that Mind's government extends to every function of man's being eliminates fear and brings healing. The wise man wrote: "The spirit of man is the candle of the Lord, searching all the inward parts of the belly." That which animates man is the enlightenment of divine Mind. There is no function of spiritual man, the embodiment of right ideas, that can possibly exist outside the activity of divine Love or fail to be governed harmoniously by this Love.

Man does not have to be changed or improved, for God perfectly conditions His idea, man. In reality he whom we term a patient knows this truth, for he reflects the one perfect consciousness. Nothing can keep us from seeing what is actually present, namely, the intelligence, health, and dominion which the Father has already bestowed on man, His idea. So Mind and its perfect ideas alone are present. There is no matter. It is most important to admit this spiritual fact. Mortal mind would have us accept its belief in matter. But its belief can never be matter — it remains mortal thought externalized.

In healing, we deal with false mental concepts, not with material conditions. As our Leader writes in the textbook: "The only fact concerning any material concept is, that it is neither scientific nor eternal, but subject to change and dissolution." The understanding that every sickness or problem is an erring thought, and that only a thought needs to be changed, breaks the mesmerism of fear, for "any material concept is . . . subject to change and dissolution."

It is utterly impossible for man to be other than completely harmonious. We are not beseeching God to give us something. We are thanking God for what He has done. God has already given His idea, man, everything that it is possible for Him to give or for man to have. The consciousness of man includes all right ideas and can contain nothing but right ideas. An article entitled "Possession," published in *The Christian Science Journal* of June, 1917, includes this statement: "It is scientifically impossible to put a wrong thought into consciousness, and there can be no imperfection in Mind, since whatever God knows is perfect and inviolable and can never be changed or altered in any way."

The belief that five and four are ten cannot be put into intelligent consciousness. Just so, any difficulty with what is termed the body is not in body, but is a belief of something untrue that never touches God's man. Hence, all error is a false belief, but is never in God or man. One destroys error when he holds to the spiritual fact which error seemingly obscures. Ignorance, uncertainty, false belief, alone believe in and accept erring suggestion. Man, the reflection of God, good, cannot yield to or be dominated by or imposed upon by animal magnetism, for he reflects the one perfect Mind, which cannot be mesmerized. The consciousness of man, God's expression, is unimpairable and uninvadable.

This is strikingly illustrated when one considers that a dream never becomes part of one's body. If you dream you are in pain, only while you dream will you feel pain. Your body remains unharmed. Awakening from the dream, you see that there is no pain to destroy. If one believes he is in pain, only while he believes it will he seem to experience pain. Yet the pain is not in matter, but in belief; and this is proved time and again when one awakens to the truth of man's harmonious, spiritual being and finds that his body and thought are untouched by the belief of pain or disease. This awakening is the appearing to human consciousness of the Christ, Truth, which always heals and saves.

A woman who had been injured when a young girl suffered for sixteen years. Reputable physicians said that the spinal nerves had been injured and that she had tuberculosis of the spine. They averred that decay had set in and that she had only a short time to remain here. When she turned to Christian Science, her practitioner secured for her a copy of *Science and Health*. Commencing earnestly to read it, she gladly accepted many statements about the perfection of God and man. The fourth day, while she was reading, it became clear to her that God had not created her diseased condition, nor did He see her in it. She glimpsed so clearly her perfection as God's child that she determined no longer to accept the difficulty, saying to herself: "If God does not see me in this condition, I refuse to believe it. He sees me as His perfect child." That day the pain in her back ceased. The next morning she was able to arise, dress herself, and walk downstairs to the astonishment of her household. This healing has proved to be permanent.

The writer has found it helpful to analyze this experience, because if the disease had been a condition in matter, if the physicians' diagnoses had been correct, if the so-called laws of *materia medica* really governed man, this ailment called incurable could not have been healed through spiritual means. The conclusion then must be that the disease was not God-created, that no law of His was regulating it, nor was any intelligent mind cognizing it, for the one Mind, God, could not and did not see it.

Since what appears as matter is but a creation of supposititious mortal thought, the individual acceptance of the general belief regarding the condition and the seeming difficulty were not two things, but one and the same — and that one a mortal belief. There is nothing else for a material condition to be, since there is no matter on which it can be delineated. Not being truly intelligent, but falsely mental, it never had actual presence, seeming to exist only when believed. When the woman accepted her God-given dominion and refused to believe the illusion, it ceased to be. It did not exist to be taken away — it needed only to be disbelieved. The intelligence of divine Mind so enlightened her consciousness that fear and false belief could not occupy thought. There was nothing to obscure the already established harmony of man's perfect being, and healing appeared to human thought.

This woman's experience helps us to see that we are not healing real disease, but through Christ, Truth, are casting out the belief that disease is real. There is in Truth no matter and no disease, for all is Mind and its harmonious, perfect, infinite ideas. The one Mind governs all. To the degree that we acknowledge its ever-present supremacy shall we prove that it governs the body not partially, but wholly, and thereby we subjugate the belief in matter to divine law. With the Psalmist we can say: "Thy word have I hid in mine heart, that I might not sin against thee." Indeed, the truth of man's spiritual being can so illumine consciousness and be so indelibly fixed in our thought that we shall not sin against God by accepting the material sense of cause and effect as real.

Since the real man is one with divine Mind, his consciousness is unalterable and cannot be influenced or dominated by suggestion, for it is scientifically impossible to put a wrong thought into

14

it. Consequently, you cannot put disease into the consciousness or identity of man. Furthermore, erring belief expressed as disease never attained presence, never entered true being; hence it does not have to be removed from man — it stays in the realm of belief and disappears when not believed.

Let us be grateful that because of our beloved Leader's revelation we are seeing more and more clearly that in Science there is no matter, that what seems to be diseased matter is erring thought, actually nonexistent, for nothing can attain presence or can possibly possess reality or existence except the divine Mind and its ideas.

WHAT COMPRISES MAN?

To ascertain what comprises man we begin with Deity, his source. Christian Science reveals God as self-existent Mind and Life, the one infinite, all-inclusive Being. Certainly God, the All-in-all, could not be in anything. On the contrary, all that really exists abides in infinite Spirit and, like its source, is purely spiritual. Because God, divine Love, is All, obviously nothing exists outside of God that can be introduced into Him or into man, His likeness, who always abides in God. Describing the inviolable nature of Deity, John has written: "This then is the message which we have heard of him, and declare unto you, that God is light, and in him is no darkness at all."

It is heartening to know that God's man does not deteriorate, because he is the unchanging likeness of his unchanging Principle. Furthermore, it is impossible for man to think a wrong or evil thought, or for a wrong concept to be put into the consciousness of man, who reflects the one infallible Mind, God. Our Leader, Mary Baker Eddy, makes clear in her writings that good does not become evil — that error does not mingle with truth or the material with the spiritual. Although these opposite qualities seem to mingle in the consciousness of man, they never really touch each other. Actually, error only seems to exist until the realization of Truth dispels evil's claim to reality and existence.

What then about the expression, "It's all in my thinking?" It is true that evil thoughts and aims are the basis of the belief in discord and disease. It is also true that evil appears to one only through the door of his own mortal sense. Naturally, the only place one can meet an unreality which seems real to him is in his own consciousness. But that which seems discordant, harmful, or limiting is but erring belief claiming to be one's thought. It is not person, place, or thing. In reality it never touches, must less becomes a part of the true consciousness of man.

The one infinite Mind is never unconscious or in any way limited. Man, reflecting Mind, the one perfect consciousness, is always awake and alert. He has no subconscious mind to harbor fear or evil, no endowed power from God with which to think a wrong thought. Moreover, in reality there is no mortal mind to introduce wrong thoughts into the perfect individual consciousness termed man. Therefore, it is unnecessary and abnormal to retain in thought old memories of past discordant, unhappy experiences and erroneous tendencies that have claimed to affect us. One can see that this abnormal retention in thought of error may give rise (in belief only) to illness, failure, and relapse in human experience. In reality it should be seen that it never is a part of man's thinking or experience. In Christian Science we do not recall, rehearse, or retain past discordant experiences or their history, whether we have overcome them or not. Like Paul, we "delight in the law of God after the inward man." Certainly our Master relinquished forever the false sense of man and continued to behold his perfect spiritual selfhood, untouched by any dream experience.

The harmony and perfection of man, God's own concept, are intact and complete. Man in the likeness of God cannot be improved. He needs nothing. How can one add to or alter the man God creates and preserves. The wise man answers, "I know that, whatsoever God doeth, it shall be for ever: nothing can be put to it, nor any thing taken from it." No evil traits and discordant propensities exist that can by any means be injected into man. What God does not include cannot be expressed by man, His reflection. While every discordant experience is a lie about man, never a part of him, in reality animal magnetism does not exist anywhere. This grand truth revealed in Christian Science can be demonstrated most helpfully in human experience.

Since God is the only communicator to man, only that can come to him or be expressed by him which is derived from his heavenly Father. Mankind believes that many factors contribute to one's human experience. To descend to this state of thought is to admit that one's being is affected by his business, his failings, or his past. Yet one's so-called mortal past never in reality becomes a part of man, and it should not limit or control thought. One should be alert to see how much one is allowing the past to influence his present thought. "But," one may ask, "how can I really surrender the past to God?" The answer is, by acknowledging that He has always owned and controlled one's being. Consequently, error has never possessed anyone's past or accomplished its claims. Paul spent no time counting his mistakes or lamenting what was actually an unreal past. He needed every moment in which to go forward, to experience the unfoldment of reality — his rightful heritage in accord with divine law. Like Paul, we are engaged in waking out of the dream of life in matter into the recognition of life in Spirit.

And what of disease? Can it be introduced into man or become a part of his body? Mrs. Eddy answers these questions when she writes in *Science and Health*, "If the body is diseased, this is but one of the beliefs of mortal mind." From this we gather that we do not behold a diseased body, but a belief of mortal mind calling itself a diseased body. Because being is subjective, human consciousness cannot perceive anything external to itself. It believes in disease first and then perceives the externalized falsity of its own believing. Disease, then, is always thought delineated. It is never a material condition, but always an erroneous mental state. Under the marginal heading, "Peremptory demands," our beloved Leader writes: "To the physical senses, the strict demands of Christian Science seem peremptory; but mortals are hastening to learn that Life is God, good, and that evil has in reality neither place nor power in the human or the divine economy." (ibid)

This illuminating passage has helped countless individuals to see the unreal nature of evil and disease. Admitting only that evil has neither place nor power in the divine economy, one may not perceive that evil has in reality neither place nor power in the

body is not material
body is idea

human economy as well. Even in the human order, one must see that disease is not in body, but merely in mesmeric belief. This is why what are termed serious ailments can be quickly cured. They do not exist in the human economy, but in erring thought, to which they have been mesmerically suggested — hence, they do not have to be destroyed as actualities. They have only to be disbelieved. Animal magnetism has no consciousness of the real. Even its symptoms are suggestions — its crafty way of deluding one into accepting its false belief in disease. But animal magnetism has no power to enter consciousness unless one accepts as real the nonexistent, or that which God did not create.

Mrs. Eddy, in *Christian Science versus Pantheism*, under the caption, "Jesus' Definition of Evil," explains the total unreality of evil and disease. She writes: "Jesus' definition of devil (evil) explains evil. It shows that evil is both liar and lie, a delusion and illusion. Therefore we should neither believe the lie, nor believe that it hath embodiment or power; in other words, we should not believe that a lie, nothing, can be something, but deny it and prove its falsity. After this manner our Master cast out evil, healed the sick, and saved sinners."

A delusion is a mental error, a misleading of the mind. An illusion is a false appearance. Neither a delusion nor an illusion is in the divine Mind, which is the Mind of man. Intelligence is conscious only of that which is true. It cannot become deluded or cognizant of a false appearance. A delusion connotes lack of intelligence. An illusion is not an actual presence even humanly — it is an erring suggestion apparent only to a false mentality mesmerically controlled.

Animal magnetism in all its pretensions is only a lie about that which is really present. It cannot engender or perpetuate fear. It cannot create disease or inject it into man's body. It mesmerically lies about man's unalterable God-given health and harmony. How grateful we are for Mrs. Eddy's disclosure of the unreal nature of animal magnetism. It helps us to destroy error not as an entity or a condition, but as a mesmeric suggestion. A friend of the writer was keenly alert to the impersonal magnetic nature of evil. If he made a mistake and recognized it, or if it was pointed out to him, he corrected it immediately. Then he went right on as though nothing had happened. He did not dwell on the error, rehearse it, or become depressed. He understood that animal magnetism in all its pretension had never reached a point of actual existence or become a part of his inviolate spiritual selfhood in the likeness of God.

How practically Paul has written: "Wherefore henceforth know we no man after the flesh; yea, though we have known Christ after the flesh, yet now henceforth know we him no more. Therefore if any man be in Christ, he is a new creature: old things are passed away; behold, all things are become new." When one's consciousness is illumined with the Christ, the ideal Truth, old things (thoughts) can indeed pass away quickly, for it is discerned that they never belonged to man. Moreover, all things are become new — that is, the Christ reveals as present now the right ideas and qualities comprising man's being. Since man is the complete representation of infinite Mind, every good is ours now and eternally. We need but to understand, claim, and enjoy all good, our divine inheritance.

A perfect idea cannot manifest imperfection. Man, therefore, cannot express or possess anything that does not stem from God, his perfect source. Individual man is Godlike in quality. In man the ideas and qualities of God are individualized and expressed. His consciousness perfectly reflects God. The presence of man really denotes the presence and activity of God's ideas. Man, the flawless expression of Deity Himself, knows and has dominion over all. Indeed, he includes every right idea and perfect attribute of his Maker. These are what comprise man.

MAN'S IMPERVIOUSNESS TO EVIL

On the lawn of the public library of a New England city stands a large stone statue. Several hundred boys used to pass this building on their way to school, and in cold weather it was quite the thing to hit the face of the statue with a snowball. Some years the snowballs would freeze, hiding the features of the statue and making it unrecognizable throughout the winter, but the warm spring sun would always melt away the frozen snow — then the face of the figure in stone would stand forth unchanged and unharmed by the winter's accumulation. The snow always remained on the outside of the statue and never penetrated the solid stone.

Christian Science explains sin and discord of every nature as never entering man's real being — indeed, they never even touch man. They are no more part of him than the snow was part of the statue. Although appearing very real during the winter of temptation — fear, self-pity, ingratitude, discouragement, and sin invariably melt under the warmth of the realization of Love's presence and control of man. Their existence is not actual, but suppositional; hence these beliefs are not in man, but only in a false sense of self. It is heartening to know that man in the likeness of God is unharmed and unimpaired by strained relationships, illness, or the lies of frustration and failure. More impervious than stone is to snow is man's spiritual being to discord or disease.

God and his creation are eternally perfect. God, divine Principle, is the source, origin, and cause of all that exists. There can be nothing beside, or outside of God, for He is all-inclusive Being. All action proceeds from and is governed by Him. Divine Love never fails for an instant to care for, bless, and guard with its own omnipotence each one of its children. Soul forever understands, delights in, and approves of its offspring — its expression. Every idea and

21

function of man's being is in order and rightly active, expressing the perfection of his unvarying, unopposable Principle.

Existing at the standpoint of perfect understanding, the real man in the likeness of divine Mind is conscious of himself as God made him. Being Mind's own idea, hence forever perfect, he is as impervious to sin, sickness, and limitation as is God Himself. Lack, false appetites, illness, sorrow, can never attach themselves to man. They belong to a mesmeric, false dream-sense of existence and are therefore unreal.

The Apostle John said: "Whosoever is born of God doth not commit sin; for his seed remaineth in him: and he cannot sin, because he is born of God." Sin is no more a part of the real man's being than a mistake is a part of mathematics. Those who are believing they have sinned and are sick, may waken to find in Science that God's man is neither a sick nor a sinning mortal. A false sense claiming to be man's consciousness is found to be both the sin and the disease, but this false sense is never man — it is erring belief. Illuminatingly, our beloved Leader, Mary Baker Eddy, says: "Jesus knew that erring mortal thought holds only in itself the supposition of evil, and that sin, sickness, and death are its subjective states; also, that pure Mind is the truth of being that subjugates and destroys any suppositional or elementary opposite to Him who is All." (*Miscellaneous Writings*)

Actually there is no error of any kind from which to be delivered, but only our belief in it to be destroyed. To yield to the attempted imposition of error, is to deny God, good and one's own true being, for when we do so, we associate evil's false claims with ourselves. The consciousness of the real man is inviolate; it cannot drift into evil; it has been and forever is impervious to error's lies. No erring mentality can attach itself to man who eternally reflects the one unerring, infallible Mind, which is God, good. Man is perfect in God, forever separate from and untouched by evil, and from this scientific basis we can solve our human problems.

Maybe an illness, an accident, or some other phase of discord presents itself, and would call itself our problem. But error is only lying about some grand spiritual truth — it has no power to act or to bring any of its illusions into our experience. Since God is omni-active good, God, Mind, is imparting to our true conscious-ness at the very moment of temptation, its glorious spiritual ideas to be utilized in the solution of what appears as our problem. Love eternally demands that we prove the present and enduring perfection of man's being, and we can demonstrate this fact in any situation.

Are we prone to try to solve our problems in the belief that they are real? Do we start with error and try to get rid of it by finding out and accounting overmuch for what is wrong in our-selves? Harmony will be established as we get rid of the belief that something is actually wrong with man. The acknowledgment of the truth of one's being as a child of God enables one gratefully to reject as unreal the erroneous belief that falsely claims identity.

Let us entertain the right idea of man as spiritual, unblem-ished, sinless, diseaseless, whole, and perfect, expressing forever the freedom, harmony, and dominion of his divine Principle, God. Humanity will then be satisfied, and find that because no false appetite, sin, or sickness ever attached itself to man, there is in reality nothing to be changed, healed, or removed. If one feels ill or discouraged, he should know that this is only a false mesmeric argument claiming to obscure his flawless spiritual being. Sin and disease are not conditions within man, but lies about him.

Christian Science breaks the mesmerism which would attach nonexistent evil to a person. John states that "a man can receive nothing, except it be given him from heaven." Can anyone know or possess a false belief, a failure, a sorrow, an illness, lack of supply, or a discordant past? No! One cannot understand or pos-sess that which is untrue, non-existent, any more than one can un-derstand or possess the misstatement that five plus five is eleven.

Error can flourish only as we give our consent. In *Science and Health* our beloved Leader writes: "What is termed matter, being unintelligent, cannot say, 'I suffer, I die, I am sick, or I am well.' It is the so-called mortal mind which voices this and appears to itself to make good its claim." The argument of suppositional mortal mind never deceives man, for he reflects the one perfect Mind, which is God. Man always thinks, feels, and acts in accord with the perfect law of God.

When confronted with family or business problems, with sin or sickness, we find that the understanding of man's imperviousness to evil in Science breaks the sense of mesmerism and brings release. When it is understood that an illness is the result of individual acceptance of that which is actually nonexistent, it can be refused admittance. When we understand our God-bestowed power to think rightly, and to reflect the one perfect Mind, we can overcome error's claim to identify itself with our consciousness. The individual who refuses to consent to mortal mind's suggestion of sickness cannot be sick. Moreover, he who understandingly clings to the present perfection of man, with no mental reservation, cannot fail to receive the evidence of his eternal harmony in his human experience.

Our beloved Leader states: "Man is incapable of sin, sickness, and death. The real man cannot depart from holiness, nor can God, by whom man is evolved, engender the capacity or freedom to sin." (*Science and Health*) Thus man is capable of imaging forth nothing less than the intelligence, harmonious action, wholeness, and perfect qualities of Almighty God Himself. Man, the individual consciousness of good, is instantly and constantly responsive to good. He is eternally cognizant of good, understands the omnipotence of good, expresses good alone, and sees only good expressed.

Man, God's spiritual idea, is undeviatingly perfect. Nowhere in her writings does our Leader connect error with man, the expression of God. The consciousness of man's sinless, spiritual selfhood, including only the good derived from God, removes from thought the belief that we can be made the medium of any sort of imperfection. And we must demand the evidence of our undefiled, joyous, harmonious, spiritual nature now.

"THESE ALSO DOETH THE SON"

In an article entitled "Christian Science" in *Miscellaneous Writings*, Mary Baker Eddy says: "By this system, too, man has a changed recognition of his relation to God. He is no longer obliged to sin, be sick, and die to reach heaven, but is required and empowered to conquer sin, sickness, and death; thus, as image and likeness, to reflect Him who destroys death and hell. By this reflection, man becomes the partaker of that Mind whence sprang the universe."

The basis of healing in Christian Science is an understanding of perfect God and of man as His reflection. Jesus referred to true identity thus: "The Son can do nothing of himself, but what he seeth the Father do: for what things soever he doeth, these also doeth the Son likewise." And what is true of Jesus' Christ-like nature is equally true of the real selfhood of each one of us. Indeed, as reflection, individual man has no choice but to show forth all the qualities and attributes of his divine Principle, "for what things soever he doeth, these also doeth the Son likewise."

There is one Being, even God. God and His idea coexist — they are inseparable. They express the infinity and unity of being in divine Science. God reflects or expresses Himself, and the emanation of His being, His reflection or expression, is termed man. There is no God without man, and man does not act apart from God. It follows that as reflection, man must do everything his source does.

On the other hand, because man expresses God, good, he can never be a medium for any phase of evil. To associate error with man is to attempt to make God responsible for it. Individuals have been healed through realizing that it is a sin against God to believe that man is sick. Man, in reality, is not committing the errors of mind and body that animal magnetism falsely attributes to him.

Moreover, he does not actually believe that he is sick, sinful, or separated from God. God's man has no ability to believe such lies. Animal magnetism lies when it claims that man is accepting sin and sickness. Contrariwise, at that very moment man is awake to the truth of his being, for he reflects the divine consciousness, which cannot be invaded.

There is one Mind, God — one voice, the voice of God. God is the only communicator to man. Error cannot, in reality, talk to man. It talks to itself, but what it appears to say is all a mesmeric claim of animal magnetism and never reaches man's consciousness. There is in reality no evil mind with a desire to do wrong or to mesmerize man. Since there is one Mind, man, Mind's idea, has no mind that can be made to accept or manifest evil, and there is no means by which error's lying suggestions can be transferred to man.

The angels, or spiritual ideas of Mind, unfold with man, who is ever at one with God. They reveal to him his present perfect being, in which every function and action is eternally harmonious. They assure him that no evil power exists that can undo man's God-decreed perfection, which is all that can be known, felt, or expressed. Man is the very evidence or witness that God is present and that His power and ability are being fully represented. As Isaiah expressed it: "I have declared, and have saved, and I have shewed, when there was no strange god among you: therefore ye are my witnesses, saith the Lord, that I am God . . . This people have I formed for myself; they shall shew forth my praise."

Then the crux of the whole matter is that reflection cannot stop or be stopped, because there is nothing outside of God to stop God. This was demonstrated in the case of a young man whom doctors had failed to heal of tuberculosis and who in his extremity turned to Christian Science. The practitioner explained that although the erection of a sky-scraper may seem to cut off the sun's ray, what really occurs is that at the point of contact, light energy is converted into heat energy — yet the light and intensity of the ray are not affected because its source, the sun, from which it derives all its activity, has not been altered. In fact the individual ray or reflection of the sun not only remains unimpaired, but may even warm and light homes and territory a hundred miles distant. The only possible way to change the ray's intensity would be to travel out to the sun and alter its course. In a similar way, the practitioner pointed out man is the unimpairable reflection of his unchanging divine Principle, God.

The teachings of Christian Science concerning matter were discussed. As the patient grasped the truth that matter is merely the externalization of mortal thought, he realized that the apparent difficulty was not a material condition, but wholly a mental error, defective thought externalized. Thus the understanding of the truth regarding spiritual reflection and the unreal nature of matter brought a change in his consciousness — an enlightened sense before which the image of mortal thought termed tuberculosis disappeared. In a short time the young man was again at work. This healing has remained permanent.

Healings like this help us to see that the harmony and perfection of man, who is the expression of God, are always present to be demonstrated. In our prayers we do not ask God to be God. God is the immutable, inviolable Principle of all being. It is impossible for God not to be God. But one may ask, "How does that help me?" The answer is that just as it is impossible for God not to be God, so it is impossible for man not to be man — the immutable, perfect man God made him to be. Man and all the ideas and functions he includes, are always Godlike. Mrs. Eddy explains this in the Christian Science textbook, where she writes: "Be firm in your understanding that the divine Mind governs, and that in Science man reflects God's government." We should always understand that the divine Mind governs, but a complete apprehension of this truth must include the fact that man reflects God's government.

It is important to recognize that there is always a perfect effect because the perfect cause is God. This line of thought may be further enlarged. The result of God being Mind is that man is alert and intelligent. The activity of infinite Spirit keeps man spiritual and pure. The effect of God being Soul is that man forever manifests the attributes and faculties of the one indestructible consciousness. The effect of God being Principle is that man is undeviatingly perfect. The effect of God being the one and only Life is that man, its expression, is vigorous and well. The activity of Truth signifies that man is righteous and infallible. The effect of God being Love is that man is fearless in the understanding of his oneness with perfect Love.

There is also a perfect effect because of God being the one all-seeing Mind. Accordingly, there is no vision but the immaculate, permanent vision of Soul, divine Mind. God's vision is forever manifested through man. Therefore, man His reflection, sees as God causes him to see, and sees all that God sees. And what has been said of man's sight, applies equally to his hearing as the reflection of the all-hearing Mind. It also applies to man's substance as the expression of the one all-inclusive Mind. God, Mind, being cognizant only of His own all-encompassing infinity, cannot know meagerness and lack — so man, His reflection, cannot know them. It follows that the affluence of man is independent of so-called material laws or conditions. His supply does not need to be acquired, but is as infinite and ever present as is God, his source. Hence, there can be no interruption, no coming or going, to man's supply. It consists of the ideas of Deity Himself. These, entertained and understood, are ever manifested humanly in all that is needful, for man is Deity's evidence of His limitless good.

Similarly, man's health is not something outside of him that he needs to gain. Neither can matter give it to him or deprive him of it. Health is a condition of divine Mind, not of matter. Hence man, Mind's reflection, must abide continuously in a state of health and harmony. Even when the deceitful senses falsely claim he is ill, man is well in Science and conscious of that fact. He ever exists harmoniously in divine Mind, God, untouched by erring human beliefs. Health, harmony, perfection of mind and body, are the eternal facts of his being.

James wrote: "If any be a hearer of the word, and not a doer, he is like unto a man beholding his natural face in a glass: for he beholdeth himself, and goeth his way, and straightway forgetteth what manner of man he was. But who so looketh into the perfect law of liberty, and continueth therein, he being not a forgetful hearer, but a doer of the work, this man shall be blessed in his deed." Are not James' words an exhortation to cognize the present perfection of our being so clearly that we keep it eternally before our thought in an earnest effort to demonstrate it? Perfection can be demonstrated because it is true. The one who really grasps his present perfection as God's own likeness is apt to talk little about it. But there will be within him an active, eager desire to live it. Furthermore, practicing man's perfection will help one to understand it better and to express more fully the fact that "in Science man reflects God's government."

How enlightenedly our beloved Leader describes man's infinite ability: "Man is God's image and likeness; whatever is possible to God, is possible to man as God's reflection. Through the transparency of Science we learn this, and receive it: learn that man can fulfill the Scriptures in every instance." (*Miscellaneous Writings*) Thus in Science the Word is made flesh, for man's perfect harmony and limitless capacity for good, which were so gloriously proved by Jesus, can be demonstrated by us here and now. And each one is greatly aided in achieving this high goal through his joyous wholehearted acceptance of the Master's perfect statement concerning reflection.

Jesus ever recognized God as the only creator, as the All-in-all. He made it clear that man is not a creator but reflection, and that as reflection he cannot be a medium for any sort of limitation or disease. But he also revealed to humanity for all time that heartening demonstrable fact that "what things soever he (God) doeth, these also doeth the Son likewise."

MAN ABIDES IN ALL-INCLUSIVE DEITY

Mrs. Eddy in *Science and Health* thus defines the word "in": "A term obsolete in Science if used with reference to Spirit, or Deity." God is not in anything. Deity cannot be localized. Where could God, the one all-inclusive Being, who fills all space, be confined?

How perfectly our Leader, Mary Baker Eddy, explains Deity's all-inclusiveness in *Unity of Good*, where she writes: "God is All-in-all. Hence He is in Himself only, in His own nature and character, and is perfect being, or consciousness. He is all the life and mind there is or can be. Within Himself is every embodiment of Life and Mind. If He is All, He can have no consciousness of anything unlike Himself; because, if He is omnipresent, there can be nothing outside of Himself."

God's creation must exist in Him. While unlocalized Deity can never be in man, God is reflected by man. Because reflection cannot be interfered with, not a single quality of God expressed by man can be interrupted or lost. As the reflection or representation of Mind, God, man must forever include every good that belongs to his Maker. There is then nothing outside himself that the real man, expressing infinite Mind, needs to grow into or acquire. Life's image is energetic, showing forth the vigor of Almighty God Himself. The son of God, Mind, does not need to gain understanding, since he is everlastingly one with infinite, alert intelligence. God's idea expresses the infallibility of Truth, the serenity of divine Love, and the stability of Principle.

When we consider the word "in," two helpful phrases to note are "in belief" and "in reality." All that is harmonious and perfect exists "in reality" and is inherent in man as God's spiritual idea. All that appears limiting or discordant is extraneous to man, and exists only "in belief." Man is well and perfect in reality, and he knows it. Irrespective of what one may seem to believe or say, man is aware of these facts, for he reflects the divine consciousness. Moses perceived that the attributes of God are individualized in man when he heard the Lord say: "I have filled him with the spirit of God, in wisdom, and in understanding, and in knowledge, and in all manner of workmanship."

Problems are not part of man. But the intelligence that solves a problem is inherent in man. Let us heed our Leader's words in *Miscellaneous Writings*: "To impersonalize scientifically the material sense of existence — rather than cling to personality — is the lesson of today." Man is forever a spiritual idea. He is not a mortal personality in trouble, in sickness, or in lack. Such seemingly inharmonious states are not conditions "in" man, but mesmeric lies attempting to hide his glorious spiritual selfhood. As a spiritual idea in Mind, man is free from the limiting belief that he is confined in a material body, is in a certain country under restrictive laws, or even in a material universe.

The truth that man is spiritual was utilized by a student of Christian Science when his small daughter became carsick. He reasoned that there is in reality no limited space, no sense of boundary, in ever-present Mind. To divine Mind there is only the sense of its own all-encompassing infinity. Because the child was a spiritual idea in Mind, not a material personality existing in finite space, she could not be subject to harm through any material belief that she was being transported from one place to another. His realization of these truths was so clear that the condition yielded almost immediately. Later, when flying, he overcame airsickness for himself by thinking along similar lines.

Fear, lack, and disease exist in belief only, not in man. The false mentality expressed as fear, lack, or disease is not present in true consciousness. Only that which is intelligent and perfect can possibly have existence in Mind or in Truth. Individual man, reflecting the divine Mind, is conscious only of good, for good alone exists and has presence. The perfection we want to see manifested is present now. Because God conditions man, we are in reality in the condition we should be in at this moment. Jesus saw the complete, sinless, diseaseless man as present now, and there is no other man either to be seen or to be acknowledged.

Matter, or mortal mind, can send no report, either good or bad, to man. Almighty God alone governs his thought. And divine Mind does not and could not permit the illusion termed an inharmonious physique or a discordant world condition to enter the real man's consciousness.

Since the real man is not in a material body, we should not act as though we were confined in one. The material concept of man is not man, but a dream sense about him. Eternally man remains God's intelligent idea, perfect even as his heavenly Father is perfect. Material sense does not change these or any other facts. For instance, if a child believes seven times seven is forty-seven and writes it on a sheet of paper, his answer is incorrect. In the same way, lack and disease are the testimony of false material sense. God, intelligent Mind, did not make and does not see them. Although believing in lack and disease may seem to externalize itself in one's experience, credence cannot bring them into real being. Error is not in God or man, not in the real body or universe — in fact, it is not "in" anything. It remains nonexistent, appearing only to itself to exist.

Just as any mistake with numbers is not in the figures, but in an erring belief about them, so any difficulty with body or business is in a belief of something untrue about them. When the body appears diseased, that appearance is but an externalized belief of mortal mind — it has not entered one's real selfhood. The man of God's creating remains perfect, untouched by erring belief, for he cannot be the medium of any sort of imperfection.

Ignorance, uncertainty, and false belief alone yield to erring thought. Intelligent thought does not and cannot yield to error. Can anyone change your knowledge of the fact that seven times seven is forty-nine? One cannot put a wrong thought into the consciousness of man any more than one can put a wrong thought into God, the infallible Mind, which man reflects. All truth, existing in intelligent Mind, is inviolate. Because man has the Mind of God, he cannot be imposed upon or wrongly influenced. An acceptance of this truth renders one immune to erroneous influences.

Animal magnetism argues that one cannot know the truth in certain situations. This aggressive suggestion has no power to make itself believed. The fact is that it is natural and effortless for man to know the truth at all times. Understanding this in every situation, one can see the need and meet it.

To return to the child who wrote seven times seven is forty-seven on the paper — after you instruct him, he erases the 47 and replaces it with a 49. In belief, erring thought delineates discord on the body, but spiritually intelligent thought will remove inharmony just as the child erased the 47. When the child wrote seven times seven is forty-seven on the paper, the truth that seven times seven is forty-nine was actually present to be demonstrated. Just so, even when mortal mind seems to externalize disease on our bodies, only the harmony and perfection of our true spiritual selfhood as God knows it are present to be proved.

In a verse that has brought solace to countless numbers, Zephaniah wrote: "The Lord thy God in the midst of thee is mighty." Wherever man is, there is God, animating, governing, and sustaining him in harmony and in perfection. Furthermore, there can be no opposition to His power and harmonious government in the midst of us. Mind, God, is the only One who moves or acts. His action is fetterless, harmonious, and perfect. Man expresses the perfect action of omni-active Mind. So all action in man is heavenly action — action as it is in heaven.

Man's substance, that is, his true intelligence, the right ideas which man already includes, constitute his supply. Man's supply then is as it is in heaven. It is not outside of man, so he does not have to acquire it, nor can he be deprived of it. As the complete idea of God, he includes his supply. There is no coming or going to supply, because it is infinite and indestructible. It is also natural to man. Like everything belonging to man, supply is eternally his, since he is the full representation of Deity, including His boundless affluence.

Eternally safe in God, man expresses the uninterruptible control of his Maker. Paul thus depicts man's security: "Now he which stablisheth us with you in Christ, and hath anointed us, is God; who hath also sealed us, and given the earnest of the Spirit in our hearts."

Throughout eternity we abide in God and He holds us perfect in His loving embrace. This unassailable oneness, this inseparability of God and His idea, man, is the unfailing basis from which to solve all our problems — that is, to destroy impersonal mesmeric beliefs with the understanding of man's present perfection.

PURGING THOUGHT

Everything God made is perfect now, and His ideas, abiding in Him, dwell together in one majestic concord. Consequently there is, in reality, nothing in God and His creation that needs to be purged. Human consciousness, however, must be purified of its false beliefs that it may demonstrate this grand spiritual truth.

To purge means to cleanse or purify, and in some instances, to clear of guilt or moral defilement. In our day the word *purge* usually signifies the ridding of a party or nation of members considered dangerous — often by brutal means. Narrowed down, it could mean the ruthless elimination of one's personal enemies. A purge is often aimed at the truth for which individuals stand, as in the case when the Pharisees wished to kill Jesus to be rid of the Christ, Truth, which he so perfectly exemplified.

A natural reaction of most of us to a purge would be, "Certainly this is one form of evil that could never activate me." But let us examine in the light of Christian Science the insidious way in which the purge method is attempting to infiltrate human thinking today. For instance, to believe in the reality of evil is to subject oneself to its machinations. Thus the one who persecutes another is laying himself open to persecution. He who indulges in hate may find himself hated, and he who believes in ruthless purging is apt to be purged himself. This applies not only in political affairs but also at home, at church, or in business — in fact, wherever individuals resort to evil methods.

In *Science and Health*, Mrs. Eddy explains: "Any human error is its own enemy, and works against itself." Because evil carries within itself the seeds of its own destruction, every endeavor to overthrow good results in the ultimate destruction of the evil purpose. While one false belief may appear to be handling many, what needs to be discerned is that the one perfect divine Mind alone is present, animating and governing all.

Our aim is to separate all error from our thought of man, to show him reverence and accord him his birthright of perfection. This is the only purge justified in the light of divine Science — namely, to purge one's own thought from every lying mesmeric belief regarding man, while acknowledging as real nothing unlike the Christ. Such a one warrants the reward whereof our Leader says in *Miscellaneous Writings*: "Through the accession of spirituality, God, the divine Principle of Christian Science, literally governs the aims, ambition, and acts of the Scientist. The divine ruling gives prudence and energy; it banishes forever all envy, rivalry, evil thinking, evil speaking and acting; and mortal mind, thus purged, obtains peace and power outside of itself."

In a business organization mortal mind may point its finger at a fellow worker and say, "He has to go." But to remove an individual does not bring spiritual progress or necessarily solve this problem. Why? Because evil is not a person, but a false belief to be seen as unreal. Nor does one necessarily heal the situation through resigning his position because a sense of injustice rankles, burdens falsely assumed seem unbearable, or error has urged a sense of inadequacy. The understanding of God's goodness routs the belief of injustice. Reliance on God and acknowledgment of His presence bring freedom from false responsibility, and the discernment of one's unlimited sufficiency as the full representation of infinite Mind, dispels the argument of inadequacy.

There are, of course, times when for his own good or that of an organization, an individual should resign or be discharged. The fallacy which one should be alert to is the prevalent belief that anyone's well-being can be enhanced merely by the removal of someone else. On the contrary, progress is always commensurate with the lifting of thought above personal sense, its methods and aims. Indeed, one can safely trust his spiritualized thinking to be externalized in what is right by knowing that God's promise is not only for him but for all. Zephaniah, after condemning the treachery in the midst of Jerusalem, declared reassuringly: "The just Lord is in the midst thereof; he will not do iniquity: every morning doth he bring his judgment to light, he faileth not."

Does one feel that he has been a victim of a purge — that he has been unjustly forced from his position or defrauded of some important assignment? He must deny this, not as an experience but as an aggressive mental suggestion attempting to draw his thought away from divine Love's perpetual control of its own. Actually, Truth and Love alone are working, furnishing us with the spiritual lesson most essential to our progress. When animal magnetism believes it has purged one — removed or defrauded him — it is really being uncovered and destroyed itself. Despite appearances, one is not a victim but has the opportunity to refute animal magnetism's claim that there is power or reality in evil's purpose. We belong to God. Therefore evil can no more control us than it can control God. His law of the unfoldment of good still governs. It has not been and cannot be thwarted. There is comfort for us in the Psalmist's words: "Promotion cometh neither from the east, nor from the west, nor from the south. But God is the judge: he putteth down one, and setteth up another."

Man reflects the unlimited intelligence of infinite Mind. Therefore one is always greater than the problem before him, for inherent in man as God's infinite idea is the intelligence that solves the problem. Because one is an individual idea of God, no one can do his work, nor can one do another's work. When we understand this, evil cannot put us out of our right place, nor put us into a wrong one. Only divine Love can move us. Progress and purging will go on until our thought is exalted above the false testimony of evil to the certain recognition that as Mind's idea we are eternally in our right place.

Furthermore, the material belief of a purge in the home, church, or business has not remedied unhappiness. Why? Because it is fallacious to feel that harmony can be obtained solely through removing a person rather than through one's spiritual-mindedness. Again, to move oneself out because someone is dominating or unjust, is often to accede to the suggestion to give error its own way. One must not purge or remove himself through an admission of his helplessness to master an inner conflict. He does not need to withdraw from certain situations or persons, but only from his own false sense of the situation and people involved. God is ever present; the one Mind is governing despite appearances, and he can know it.

There are times when it is right for one to change. A false sense of relationship or responsibility should not impel one's actions. But one should not first decide to go or stay and then work to have Principle support him in a humanly outlined plan. Nor should he permit fear, impatience, resentment, or human will to move him to a decision. Actually, man is not faced with a decision, for he reflects the divine Mind, which knows all and therefore acts immediately and unerringly. Working thus and listening to no voice but God's, one will find intelligence and love alone moving him to necessary human decisions.

How wonderful to have learned in Christian Science that God, who creates all, also holds all His ideas in the right relationship to each other. One idea of God could not encroach upon, conflict with, or prevent the right unfoldment of another idea. Because every relationship stems from divine Love, it must be enlightening and liberating, never reactionary or restrictive. Thus what appear as discordant human relationships are not external, but are erroneous thought conditions to be purged from within. The seeker after Truth knows that to become uplifted in thought is his real demonstration. Then ever-present good, which has seemed absent, becomes so real that he loses his sense of unhappiness. The burden lifts because his thought has been illumined or anointed with the Christ, Truth, and Isaiah's words are proved true: "And it shall come to pass in that day, that his burden shall be taken away from off thy shoulder, and his yoke from off thy neck, and the yoke shall be destroyed because of the anointing."

The spiritualization of one's thought is not complete until it is purged of every erroneous world belief. One should affirm with no mental reservation that he is a child of divine Love, that he is ever loved by his Father-Mother God, from whom he inherits all good. Joyously one can declare that as a spiritual idea, dwelling forever in God, he is not subject to a past or a future, but only to God's law of good. Firmly one should own that he has no weaknesses, but that he is strong at every point, that he is God's infinite idea, unlimited in intelligence and ability, ever conscious of his radiant being as a complete representation of all-inclusive Mind.

One praying thus contemplates man's spiritual nature with the desire of becoming conscious of the completeness of his own true selfhood. Then he earnestly strives to live with his prayer. And in purging his consciousness of false worldly beliefs and opening it to the one infinite presence, he will find his body, his church, and his affairs being purged of all inharmony. Indeed, the Christ is here, illumining the consciousness of all men, purging thought of all evil, and glorifying God, good.

CAN CRITICISM HEAL?

The goal of a Christian Scientist is to abide in a healing consciousness. The Psalmist thus expresses this aspiration: "Create in me a clean heart, O God; and renew a right spirit within me . . . Then will I teach transgressors thy ways; and sinners shall be converted unto thee."

To attain this consciousness sought by the Psalmist, one must refrain from destructive criticism, which does not heal. True criticism, however, discovers excellencies as well as defects. One of the functions of criticism is to evaluate events, and this should lead to correction and healing. Consequently, one does not need to forego criticism. It is only destructive criticism from which he should abstain. Judging or examining in Christian Science is founded upon the basic truth that the divine Mind beholds all things as perfect as it conceived them. And because the one wholly good Mind is the only Mind of man, there is in reality no mind with the desire to criticize destructively.

Our motive in discerning thought is always to heal. Truly to recognize error is to see its unreal nature so clearly that one puts it out of thought. Criticism that is synonymous with true judgment impersonalizes evil, always reducing it to a false belief. It acknowledges that everything which has presence is good and refuses to let error hide good. On the other hand, destructive criticism inflates error. It tends to make real to us what we dislike. One given to such criticism needs enlightenment — then the unreal will no longer seem real to him. Mrs. Eddy explains this in *Science and Health*, where she writes, "You command the situation if you understand that mortal existence is a state of self-deception and not the truth of being." Only as we are willing to admit that whatever appears annoying is a state of self-deception — mesmeric suggestion individually accepted — are we in a position to "command the situation."

A practitioner once said to one who was critical of his friend, "You are hard on yourself about Bill." Error was attempting to dethrone the Christ in his consciousness by having him regard Bill's errors as real. Those who criticize adversely are not seeing the Christ. They are hard on themselves because they are not truly seeing their brother, but mortal mind's defective concept of him.

To cast aspersions on the acts, or to impugn the motives of another, is not the Christ-way of destroying error, but animal magnetism's method of having one retain it. The admission in thought of the failure of another, reacts upon us and weakens our defense against evil. A right thought extended to him in an hour of need, mentally or audibly as divine Mind directs, helps him and us. Again, it is a fallacy to believe that one evil thought is equal in power to one thought of good. If an individual's consciousness seems to consist largely of evil thoughts, this need not be discouraging. The evil is mesmeric, and is not actually present. False beliefs can never affect or enter the consciousness of God's man. One right thought is sufficient to dispel them, so omnipotent is Truth.

If a member erred in a branch church some years ago, credence should not be given to the error now. Let us ask ourselves: "What are we expecting to see — the same error that was formerly manifested, or the real man who never lapsed into evil?" We shall progress in proving our own oneness, or unity, with God when we do not identify error with man.

Businessmen sometimes give a single error power. Adverse criticism of an individual may culminate in attributing the unprofitable or inharmonious functioning of a useful enterprise to his one error of judgment. It is much better to know that no error can hinder or obstruct what is right. Such thinking finds that no loss or retrogression can occur under Love's intelligent government. Indeed, there cannot be an incomplete transaction in God's universe. All is subject to His infallible control. In reality every right activity, or transaction, is going on in heaven. The only power that can act is good, the only law is God's unopposable law of justice.

The only participants are God's children, at one with the Father, impelled by Love, and enlightened by Mind.

The following demonstrates that the one who lives Christian Science himself is most successful in helping others. A patient was needlessly voicing discord. The practitioner remonstrated, "You have talked error for twenty minutes," but this remark did not deter her. Sensing his own irritation, the practitioner saw that being annoyed was not abiding in a healing consciousness. Quickly correcting his thought, he was able to help his patient, and this instance has been to him a salutary reminder on other occasions.

It is absurd to be disturbed by another's mistake. Man is impervious to evil. Knowing this, one is immune to every upsetting tendency or discordant reaction that would tempt him to accept mortal mind's unjust criticism. Indeed, he knows that the same error which makes his brother act unwisely, would mesmerize him into believing the wrong-doing. He rejoices that animal magnetism can neither create nor externalize any such lie as appears to argue. The one perfect consciousness, God, has no sense of evil. It is inviolable. This infallible Mind is the only Mind. God's man is cognizant only of good. It is impossible for man to think an evil thought, and it is heartening to know that evil thinking is always false, never attaining reality.

When anyone who is disturbed or feels unduly critical learns that only his own thought needs to be corrected, he gains assurance. Why? Because he has accurately reduced the problem to a suggestion arguing to his thought. He can now handle it effectively, for he always has dominion over his thinking. Herein lies the effectiveness of sound criticism, which sees through the pretense of error and refuses to have thought diverted from the ever-present Christ.

One always deals, not with external conditions, but with what appears as his own sense of things. If then, error seems real to him, and if he wishes to be a good critic, he should analyze or examine himself. When we judge ourselves from a human standpoint, the result may be unsatisfactory — yet spiritual sense helps us not to become embarrassed or depressed, but to see that evil, even when it claims to be our own thought, has never reached the point of existence. The inspiration which discloses the suggestion as unreal and mesmeric enables us to correct it and then go right on as though nothing had happened.

If we examine our true selfhood — that is, if we see ourselves as divine Mind sees us — we shall find the harmony, holiness, and perfection with which God has endowed man. True criticism demands scientific and constant adherence to good, to man's unblemished perfection as a child of God. We have God-derived power to hold thought to good, to apprehend and love what is actually present, both in others and in ourselves. Paul sums up true criticism thus: "Examine yourselves, whether ye be in the faith; prove your own selves. Know ye not your own selves, how that Jesus Christ is in you?"

But the query may come, How can I straighten out a situation external to myself merely through self-examination and righteous judgment? The answer is that what are termed external events do not control the human consciousness which is governed by the Christ — rather, it is the other way around. Human consciousness is externalized in what is termed human experience or unfoldment. When one begins earnestly to correct every thought unlike the Christ, he is knowing and utilizing God's thoughts, which cannot fail to dispel error. Eyesight has been improved and stubborn illnesses have yielded as individuals have forsaken a falsely critical sense which sees another's error as real and have honestly examined and corrected their own thought.

No good is ever disturbed. When we are annoyed by evil manifested through another, the annoyance needs to be healed, for when our consciousness is illumined with the Christ, it sees error as powerless and no part of man. In God's kingdom there is nothing to cause irritation. Mrs. Eddy writes: "The Revelator tells us of 'a new heaven and a new earth.'" And she adds this question: "Have you ever pictured this heaven and earth, inhabited by beings under the control of supreme wisdom?" (*Science and Health*)

To look out on the universe with the Mind of Almighty God is to behold all there is to be known or expressed. The one Mind is seen to be governing all, and good to be unfolding according to divine law. The one all-embracing divine presence precludes the actual existence of anything else. Everything that really exists emanates from God and is good. We indulge in unworthy criticism because we have been deluded into accepting mortal mind's belief that something besides good is taking place.

Spiritualized thought is so anchored in the infinite goodness of God that it demonstrates the unreality of evil. This is the scientific evaluation, the righteous judgment or true criticism, which casts errors of belief out of oneself and heals.

"THAT WHICH YE HAVE"

Inasmuch as human environment is but the externalization of thought, it can be improved as thought is corrected and spiritualized. Similarly, the apparent lack of a home is not primarily a material condition, but the outward expression of a general belief.

No one would ever think of the multiplication table or any part of it as not being present or available. When we affirm that God is omnipresent, we acknowledge that all that exists is in His omnipresence now. All the ideas and resources of Mind must be present where we are. Moreover, neither God's eternal presence, wherein is all good, nor Mind's constant, unimpaired productiveness has ever been set aside in any apparent lack of home.

The real man lives in divine Mind, in divine consciousness. Home, being the consciousness of harmony, is forever included in man's being. Hence the real man can never be without his home, nor separated from it. It is as natural to him as are honesty and justice. Today mortals can understand and prove more fully, because of the revelation of Christian Science, the harmony, continuity, safety, security, and adequacy of man's home in the kingdom of Mind. In the words of a hymn:

> *For Thou, within no walls confined,*
> *Dwellest with them of humble mind;*
> *Such ever bring Thee where they come;*
> *And where Thou art they find their home.*

A Christian Scientist was faced with the need of finding a home in a large eastern city where the housing shortage was reported to be very acute. While working on the problem, he concluded that the only solution lay in relying wholly upon God, who does not know meagerness or lack — that because divine Mind knows only affluence and abundance, he, as God's idea, must be conscious of these verities. As he listened to the angel thoughts of God acquainting him with what man, God's expression, possesses, this passage came to him with great clarity: "Now therefore perform the doing of it; that as there was a readiness to will, so there may be a performance also out of that which ye have. For if there be first a willing mind, it is accepted according to that a man hath, and not according to that he hath not."

Then he reasoned that because man already reflects every quality of God, he exists in a state of abundance, not of need. The Scientist saw that his only need was to understand and accept as real what he spiritually possessed as a son of God in order to have the evidence of it, "so there may be a performance" — that is, an expression — "out of that which ye have." As he strove to accept only spiritual realities, his consciousness was illumined with glorious truths about home. He became confident that they would be evidenced "according to that a man hath," and that his experience could not be determined by "that he hath not," or by what mortal mind falsely claimed he lacked.

Several acquaintances mentioned that the only possible way to find a home was to know the owner of a building, because owners were allocating apartments that became available to their relatives and close friends. While he was not acquainted with any owner, he did know that all that truly is, belongs to God. The Psalmist wrote: "The earth is the Lord's and the fullness thereof." Moreover, there was no nepotism or partiality in divine Mind. Was he not related to God as His own beloved son? And was not divine Love caring for him and unfailingly supplying his needs? This verse of a hymn proved uplifting:

> *Pilgrim on earth, home and heaven are within thee,*
> *Heir of the ages and child of the day.*
> *Cared for, watched over, beloved and protected,*
> *Walk thou with courage each step of the way.*

Because man includes the idea of home, the student refused to think of himself as needing one. He clung understandingly to the spiritual fact that his true sense of home, his abiding consciousness of harmony, could never be dethroned or affected by what a group of mortals falsely believed. He had the assuring statement by our Leader, Mary Baker Eddy: "The infinite will not be buried in the finite; the true thought escapes from the inward to the outward, and this is the only right activity, that whereby we reach our higher nature." (*The First Church of Christ, Scientist, and Miscellany*)

The student turned away from interviews, at which hopelessness was stressed, with the thought that there was no reality in the mesmerism that seemed to be binding these people. But he wakened to see that if he regarded man as mesmerized, he was believing in mesmerism. Then he declared that man, the image of God, could not be mesmerized any more than could God, for man ever reflects the one infallible Mind.

God gives consciousness of home, and since there is but one Mind, there is no mind which can be conscious of homelessness. Man, reflecting the one perfect Mind, must be conscious of his brother man as provided by God with what constitutes home. Moreover, as the child of God, he rejoices in seeing man expressing this spiritual fact of his being. As these better concepts of God and man were utilized, helpfulness and assistance were forthcoming, and information came from an unexpected, unsolicited source which led to his securing an apartment.

Christian Scientists do not work to demonstrate material things. Rather do they work to apprehend and utilize already established spiritual truths which, in the degree they are apprehended, are externalized in what is humanly needful. One can really demonstrate only that which actually exists and is bestowed on man by God. It is wonderful to know that one cannot seek any spiritual good that man does not already possess, whether it be health, supply, happiness, or home, for all are inherent in man's being as the idea of God. Understandingly to accept these verities as one's own, brings to light the evidence of them, for there must be "a performance also out of that which ye have." Man is ever under the law of Love, never subject to so-called material conditions.

The divine decree for man is expressed in Love's ceaseless provision, and is unalterable and unassailable. God is always God, forever our loving Father. Nor has reflection stopped. Man is eternally active, reflecting God's being. There is never a moment when God is not expressed or when man fails to express — that is, to possess as reflection — every one of God's qualities. Man abides continually in a heavenly state of consciousness. Indeed, these heartening words of Mrs. Eddy are as applicable to Christian Scientists now as the day she penned them: "Like the verdure and evergreen that flourish when trampled upon, the Christian Scientist thrives in adversity; his life is a life-lease of hope, home, heaven . . ." (*Miscellany*)

CHANGING CONSCIOUSNESS
AND EVIDENCE

God, Spirit, who created all, comprehends all to be as spiritual and perfect as He made it. The harmony and perfection of man, the expression of God, is intact, unopposable, and everlastingly evident. To the all-knowing Mind and man in His likeness, everything in God's universe is present, harmonious, and unchangeable. If everything that exists is perfect and eternally evident to infinite Mind, and to the real man in the likeness of divine Mind, it is obvious that the spiritual evidence of the harmony and wholeness of God's creation does not need to be and cannot be improved upon, and in reality there is no other evidence.

It is only erring thought, the false evidence of the material senses regarding man, that needs to be changed. False concepts of man are changed, not by heeding what dogma, tradition, or material sense testimony says about him, but by understanding the real man's glorious spiritual selfhood as forever including every right idea and faculty.

It was Jesus' correct view of man that changed false evidence and enabled him to heal the sick. Like Jesus, you and I, as sons of God, omniscient Mind, do not lack the intelligence to discern what man is, or the faith that the spiritual understanding we reflect dispels the erring sense testimony that would obscure the present perfection of God's spiritual creation. If we seem unable to speak to disease with the authority of Jesus, we can reject the lying evidence of the senses and, as the following experience illustrates, acknowledge the spiritual evidence ever at hand until the realization follows which changes false evidence and heals.

A Christian Science nurse was caring for a small boy who cried constantly and loudly complained of the pain stemming from a seemingly serious spinal disorder. After prayerful thought, she showed the youngster that if he could not cease crying, he could at least stop voicing error. She said, "You are able to talk, and when you do, you should voice the truth about yourself, for to voice error is to accept it, and such acceptance appears to increase it." She assured him that as divine Love's spiritual, perfect child, he was well and happy, and that these truths were what he really wanted to think and express. "Moreover," she said, "try to understand and accept the truths you think and speak."

The child, who was most cooperative, said, "I'll stop crying as soon as I can, and beginning right now I'll declare the truth and not voice error again." He did just this. The crying lessened at once, and in a few days both the crying and the pain entirely ceased. In slightly over a week the healing was complete. We, like this child, are sometimes faced with the necessity of controlling our thought when sickness, lack, and sorrow present themselves. Actually they can become part of our experience only through our acquiescence in them, and they go out of it through our repudiation of them.

Inherent in each individual is the love of the good and true. Equally inherent in everyone, in any situation, is the power to think rightly, to reflect the divine Mind by accepting as real only those thoughts which emanate from Mind and are good and true. One can also reject the undesirable and untrue whenever error aggressively suggests them. In this control of one's thinking through spiritual understanding, lies his dominion.

Animal magnetism diabolically claims that when one needs to, he cannot acknowledge his present spiritual perfection. If this claim is accepted by the individual, he consents to contend for the unreal evidence of disease. One acceding to such a suggestion may even regard lack and discord as real, and man's sufficiency and harmony, which are a present fact, as a theory. In this deluded mental state, one appropriates what he does not want, does not need to have, and in reality cannot possess. He resists his own harmony and dominion instead of resisting with the strength of Spirit the error that is trying to obscure them. He does this because he has listened to the testimony of the material senses that falsely claims to be true, instead of holding to the spiritual evidence which is ever present, and that unfailingly silences every mesmeric lie.

A piece of paper cannot prevent us from erasing a wrong sum written on it and replacing it with the correct figures. Similarly, nothing that claims to be in the material body can withstand enlightened, spiritualized thought. Such thinking inevitably erases the mental error called disease delineated upon the body and replaces it with the spiritual fact.

An illuminating passage from our textbook, shows us how rightly to evaluate false evidence. It reads: "Any supposed information, coming from the body or from inert matter as if either were intelligent, is an illusion of mortal mind — one of its dreams. Realize that the evidence of the senses is not to be accepted in the case of sickness, any more than it is in the case of sin." And Jeremiah wrote: "Be not afraid of their faces; for I am with thee to deliver thee." Deliver us from what? From accepting as real mortal mind's presentation, which attempts to obscure the perfection of man that is evident to spiritual-mindedness.

We now see that the evidence to be changed is material consciousness, actually only an illusory mode of thought. Because mortal mind and matter combine as one, the belief and the so-called discordant condition are not two things, but one and the same thing. Discord never exists apart from mental acquiescence in it. The belief *is* the disease. Moreover, it is a falsely mental error, actually non-existent; hence it must yield as Christ, Truth, dispels the erring belief in disease. The recognition that there is no material condition to be overcome, but only an erring, mesmeric thought to be rejected through spiritual understanding, destroys fear. Seeing and claiming the harmony and perfection that are present and evident to spiritual sense, will bring them to light humanly.

Armed with these facts, the individual who turns to Christian Science for healing is on sure ground. He will find his chief difficulty to be material-mindedness, to which unrealities seem real. Under the spiritual illumination gained, dark errors of belief — worry, self-centeredness, self-pity, resentment, greed, and fear — that have seemed to obscure the harmony at hand, must recede and disappear. And as they do, harmony of thought will be manifested in a more harmonious sense of body.

Does one approach a problem as though it were real and part of his being? Let him rather begin with the perfection of Deity and acknowledge God's presence and unfailing love. As he thus prays to know and do good, his consciousness will be illumined with an understanding of God's goodness and what man in His image already is and possesses. Such a one will judge progress, not by material symptoms or mortal mind standards, but by improvement of thought. The experience of the writer and of others whom he has known, has been that when spiritualization of thought, instead of physical healing, has been earnestly sought, the enrichment desired has been attained and evidenced in peace of mind and harmony of body. One cannot improve or change human consciousness without changing the outward evidence, for they are not two things, but one and the same thing. The student who follows our Leader's positive, infallible rule, stated in *Miscellaneous Writings*, will surely succeed. There she states: "Holding the right idea of man in my mind, I can improve my own, and other people's individuality, health, and morals."

But to one in need the question may arise: how quickly may consciousness and evidence be changed? It can only be answered that it is not time that is required, but enlightenment. Since in reality there is no matter, and only erring belief needs to be changed, healing can come as quickly as one can change a thought, and Jesus so proved. Because Christ, Truth, can come to human consciousness and change thought instantly, one may awaken from the dream of sickness in a moment. It is this spiritually-illumined consciousness, in which the earnest Christian Scientist seeks to abide, that instantly dispels darkened material beliefs.

Speaking of Jesus' works, our Leader writes in *Unity of Good*: "He annulled the laws of matter, showing them to be laws of mortal mind, not of God. He showed the need of changing this mind and its abortive laws. He demanded a change of consciousness and evidence, and effected this change through the higher laws of God."

This higher law of God is always present and operating. Although human beliefs and traditions may argue to us that man is other than the pure, satisfied, harmonious, and holy idea of God, the truth is that man's true identity is undefiled and spiritual. Christ, Truth, enables one to declare and know that he is the son, or idea, of God, with God-bestowed ability to represent divine Life's unfettered, spontaneous, joyous living.

In a beautiful and inspired Bible verse Hosea has written: "In the place where it was said unto them, Ye are not my people, there it shall be said unto them, Ye are the sons of the living God."

WHAT YOU THINK COUNTS

Some years ago an experienced practitioner and I were discussing the problem of the unreceptive patient and other problems that occur in the practice of Christian Science. At that time I was unduly impressed with the resistance to Truth arguing to many seeking Christian Science help. When I mentioned this, the practitioner said: "Why give power to what any negative mortal mind thinks? What *you* think counts." The practitioner then explained that the thoughts we reflect from God, what we think of spiritual truth, is the determining factor always.

I had often thought: "How am I going to help this patient with a few good thoughts? He is thinking about ninety percent negative, material thoughts." Then I grasped two salient points. First, that a wrong thought is not equal in power to a right one. I had been judging on a quantitative instead of a qualitative basis. I had failed to cognize the power of a spiritual thought emanating from divine Mind. Secondly, I saw that erroneous thoughts are really not part of man's consciousness. They do not contain one iota of reality, but spiritual thoughts are real and substantial.

I recalled that Joshua exhorted the children of Israel not to serve the false gods of other nations, but to cleave to the Lord; and he assured them, "One man of you shall chase a thousand." And often I have paraphrased his words and have realized that one right, spiritual thought will rout a thousand wrong, material ones.

Yet someone might declare: "The above is very clear, but I am not certain how I can help another when I do not have an opportunity to talk with him. In other words, what is the *modus operandi* of absent treatment by which my prayer can benefit another?" The answer involves perceiving that in Christian Science we resolve conditions into thoughts, and then replace erroneous thoughts with spiritual ideas. We are really dealing not with people, but with the erroneous beliefs trying to control their thinking. And we can accept or reject those erroneous beliefs in proportion to the spiritual enlightenment of our own thought.

To illustrate, let us assume you are sitting in your living room with a friend. It is twilight, and you say, "I wish to read this article," and you turn on a strong overhead light. This light enables not only you, but also your friend to read. Neither had a darkness of his own. No, there was only one darkness, and one bright light dispelled it. Two lights were not required to dissipate the one darkness. The one bright light sufficed.

Correspondingly, when a man who is ill or in trouble seeks help from a Christian Scientist, the error is really the dark belief handling that man and not the person. Freedom will be demonstrated if the false claim, calling itself sickness or trouble and arguing to the patient, is destroyed. The same dark belief which is attempting to mesmerize the patient will, in turn, endeavor to deceive the Scientist. But it is not the man's or the Scientist's belief; it is one belief of mortal mind trying to mesmerize the thought of both.

Now just as the light in the living room banishes the one darkness, so the light of the Christ illumining the Scientist's consciousness is certain to destroy the one dark belief and free his patient. How clear it is that what *we* think of spiritual truth counts.

Jesus beheld the perfect man in his own consciousness. His thought was so illumined with the Christ that those within its radius who were receptive could no longer believe in or manifest sickness. How we long to emulate his works! But we must see that we can improve our thought only in our own consciousness.

To Deity everything is subjective. God's ideas remain within the consciousness of the infinite Mind which authors them, for there can be nothing external to infinite, all-inclusive Mind or to its perfect reflection, man. And all that mortal mind, the counterfeit of divine Mind, can possibly possess is its own concepts or false beliefs. It cannot create or experience anything external to itself.

Consequently, even humanly we are not confronted with discord or situations existing "out there," external to our thought. What appears as "out there" is right here, within consciousness. So all we are ever called upon to deal with are our own concepts over which, of course, we can exercise complete dominion.

How comforting to learn that human thought isn't affected by incidents occurring in a universe external to itself! Phenomena appearing in the world really take place within human thought, for humanity feels, sees, and hears its own thoughts. Our Leader, Mrs. Eddy, clarifies this for all time where she writes: "Everything is as real as you make it, and no more so. What you see, hear, feel, is a mode of consciousness, and can have no other reality than the sense you entertain of it." (*Unity of Good*)

As Christian Scientists we are heartened by this truth and endeavor constantly to bear it in mind. We change what appear to be outward conditions by changing our thinking about them, reducing them to thought and replacing them in consciousness with spiritual ideas. Doing so, we find ourselves exercising our God-given dominion over our bodies, situations, and, in fact, over all our affairs. The above elucidates the importance of our thinking, for one glimpse of spiritual truth is often sufficient to heal a case of sickness or to resolve a discordant situation claiming an extended persistency.

A Christian Scientist in the business world often demonstrates that his spiritual thinking counts. He is alert to acknowledge that there is one right purpose in business affairs, that of divine Principle, which is always just. As God's individual idea he realizes he is working for God and that his real activity is to express His qualities. He knows that he is subordinate only to the law of God. And he perceives that what he thinks determines his progress, his career, his salvation itself.

Why do not some businessmen manifest greater success? It is because they think forces are operating that can resist progress, induce frustration, or engender delays. Failure stems from not recognizing that they can counteract stagnation, frustration, and delays with spiritual thoughts that really count. You may consume hours thinking about your business, sometimes at the expense of neglecting what is more important — to know yourself as God's complete expression. You include your business in your thought, and therefore you are in a position to have dominion over it. As you come to understand what you really are, you can demonstrate that you eternally have dominion over your own thinking.

Many in business and the professions want to accomplish big things, but how preferable it is to desire to do right things! God's man is inherently successful in expressing God's qualities. You can prove that as God's idea you are bigger than any human situation. With God's help you can accomplish what is right. You should desire to be so conscious of your oneness or unity with God that you actually feel enlightened and empowered by Deity Himself.

Realizing that man's possibilities for good are limitless, you will work more freely and more joyously. If you are in business or a profession, it is well to take time to understand man's glorious, unlimited selfhood — your true selfhood. In proportion as you do, you will handle problems intelligently and make decisions unerringly. You will be equipped to master new facets of your activity creditably. You will sense that divine Principle, which is just, judges every performance. There is in reality no mortal mind to believe in or accept injustice. The law of the unopposable unfoldment of good alone is in operation, and you can be conscious of that fact.

You really do not need to acquire opportunity for expression, for man is the full representation of intelligent Mind, and includes all its ideas and the ability to express them. When you know that this is so, you will do less looking to a place, to a position, or to people for progress. You will bring progressive, dynamic, spiritual qualities to your relationships and to your position. You will be endued with power from on high and will triumph over untoward situations. Why? Because you have prayerfully listened to God. He has given you spiritual ideas which will demonstrate that what you think counts.

In like manner when healing sickness or dealing with relationship problems, you work primarily in your own consciousness. Error might attempt to resist the clarification of your own thinking — it might even argue against your ability to control your thought. But as Mind's reflection you can express only what is right. Understanding this you will think what you need to think in every situation. And you do not need to accept erroneous suggestions of any kind. Through spiritual understanding you gain control of your thought and realize your God-given dominion.

In helping others you rise above the belief that you are dealing with a finite, personal mind that can harbor both good and evil thoughts. You recognize that the one wholly good Mind is not only yours to reflect, but is also the Mind of your patient. Actually then, he does not think a wrong thought, and even when he appears to do so, error does not become any part of his true consciousness. That is why one struggling with a belief of sickness can be healed quickly.

Regardless of what a patient, or mortal mind, tells you or of what the situation appears to be, you can claim the truth. Erroneous suggestions are unsupported by Principle, for back of them there is really nothing but mere belief. On the other hand, back of your declarations of Truth is Almighty God. The patient isn't really believing or voicing error. Mortal mind is simply attempting to act as his consciousness and further its false claim.

The time is at hand to deny erring sense testimony and to exercise your divinely bestowed prerogative to nullify sickness and discordant relationship problems through spiritualized thinking, to prove your God-given dominion thus described by our Leader in the textbook: "Man, created by God, was given dominion over the whole earth." And a distinct aid in demonstrating your dominion is intelligently to claim that the words of Truth that God puts into your mouth and heart really do count. As Eliphaz said to Job: "Thou shalt also decree a thing, and it shall be established unto thee: and the light shall shine upon thy ways."

The prophets and apostles had unbounded faith and trusted the truths God had revealed to them. And of Jesus' faith in the divine Word, Mrs. Eddy writes: "Our Master said, 'Heaven and earth shall pass away, but my words shall not pass away;' and Jesus' faith in Truth must not exceed that of Christian Scientists who prove its power to be immortal." (*Miscellaneous Writings*)

The spiritual truths we live and think do count, for Christian Science treatment is the Word of God. It carries with it the presence, power, and activity of God. It is the practice of the law of life and harmony. It heals quickly and cannot be reversed. All the power that exists is in divine Mind, and by living in accord with the law of God, we reflect that power. Yes, our human ability to reflect the divine power is unlimited. And our goal is so to reflect it that these immortal words of the widow, whose son Elijah raised from the dead, may be said of us: "Now by this I know that thou art a man of God, and that the word of the Lord in thy mouth is truth."

GAINING DOMINION OVER REACTIONS

In working with people over a period of years, I have noticed that their reactions to situations or to others may result in difficulties, in enmities, and even in ailments. I have found too that people manifest peace and poise when they joyously accept and willingly demonstrate man's God-bestowed imperviousness to evil. From these experiences, I have learned in a measure to say quietly and firmly to myself, "I do not need to react to that lying suggestion." And my conviction has been strengthened that when one understands and applies the truth of man in God's image, he cannot be made to react unconsciously or adversely to any phase of evil.

Viewing from a Christianly scientific standpoint the problem of gaining dominion over reactions, we begin with one all-inclusive Mind. This one, omniactive Mind, God, is not affected by anything external to itself because nothing is acting outside of it. Consequently, as we become conscious of our oneness with or inseparability from infinite perfect Mind, we too shall express freedom from irritation.

Our example is Christ Jesus, who left the world with its wrong thinking and illusions, completely out of his reckoning and declared: "I came forth from the Father, and am come into the world: again, I leave the world, and go to the Father." It is evident that his strength lay in a conscious sense of his unity with God, for he said: "He that sent me is with me: the Father hath not left me alone; for I do always those things that please him." Like our Master, we should be governed by divine Love alone, whose impulsion is peaceful, restful, harmonious.

In demonstrating our dominion over reactions, we do not overlook the claim that reactions are essential. Newton's law of motion reads, "For every force there is an equal and opposite force or reaction." What Newton has said about mechanics prevails quite generally in human thought.

Mrs. Eddy was cognizant of this, for in writing helpfully of action, reaction, temper, friction, and equanimity, she says: "We should remember that the world is wide; that there are a thousand million different human wills, opinions, ambitions, tastes, and loves; that each person has a different history, constitution, culture, character, from all the rest; that human life is the work, the play, the ceaseless action and reaction upon each other of these different atoms." And she adds, "Then, we should go forth into life with the smallest expectations, but with the largest patience; with a keen relish for and appreciation of everything beautiful, great, and good, but with a temper so genial that the friction of the world shall not wear upon our sensibilities; with an equanimity so settled that no passing breath nor accidental disturbance shall agitate or ruffle it." (*Miscellaneous Writings*) Here the question may arise, Are all reactions voluntary? Christian Science teaches that they are. No disturbance is ever from without. No situation or person can irritate you. Only you can disturb you, and then only in belief.

But just as a building with no roof has no protection against dust, rain, snow, or anything in the material atmosphere, so a human consciousness that is not doing constructive, spiritual thinking has no protection against what is in the atmosphere of mortal thought. This explains why some people do things they do not intend to do. They say things they do not mean to say. In belief, they have become victims of something that is going on in mortal thought, whether it be irritation, disease, or immoral behavior.

Common consent is a source of contagion not only of disease, but also of other phases of mortal thought. What interests us is our superiority to error's attempt to control our thought. We can order our own lives from the basis of our inseparable unity with divine Principle, God.

Now, to consider a phase of reaction — stimulus: right stimulus is never absent, for Mind stimulates man. And that stimulation is harmonious and strengthening. Our Leader declares: "The fact that Truth overcomes both disease and sin reassures depressed hope. It imparts a healthy stimulus to the body, and regulates the system. It increases or diminishes the action, as the case may require, better than any drug, alterative, or tonic. Mind is the natural stimulus of the body, but erroneous belief, taken at its best, is not promotive of health or happiness." (*Science and Health*)

Wrong thoughts tend to stimulate the body adversely, cause the organs to act or react discordantly, thereby giving rise to some phase of disease. In such cases, the practitioner works to calm the thought of his patient with spiritual truth.

Self-will has a driving, upsetting tendency that may be disturbing to the functions and organs of the body. Self-will wants what it wants when it wants it. If it does not get it, it is apt to be disturbed. Often it is our self-will that is irritated and offended by another's actions. As we learn to silence our will in little things, we become not only more humble, but also more harmonious. Certainly to pray to God, but still listen to our willful desires instead of allowing the divine influence to change and spiritualize our thought, is to retain, not destroy, self-will. The way to overcome self-will is to wait for God to move us; really to heed the Father's voice.

When we set our heart on a certain situation or possession, at the same instant we open our mental doors to possible disappointment should the desire remain unfulfilled. This is evil's attempt to hide from us our completeness and satisfaction derived from Spirit, God. Oh, to be so removed from selfish desires and personal sense that we claim and express no will but the Father's! This was Jesus' strength and his joy too. And it can be ours.

One may ask, "What is my reaction to what mortal mind avers is my human past?" The past is one of mortal mind's ways of trying to cause dejected thoughts. Error may argue that lack of education, background, or success can limit our progress. We should remember that whatever claims to have happened in the past cannot interfere with our inherent power to recognize and demonstrate our perfect selfhood now.

There is, moreover, no law of mortal mind that can repeat a moral deviation or a disease. Error is a false mesmeric claim which did not actually occur the first time. What God did not give us — what in reality we never had — cannot repeat itself. Animal magnetism would like to divert our thought from truth by keeping alive what never really occurred. We must refuse to dwell on the belief of a discordant past.

Through Science we can prove that at all times and in all places we are one with alert, clear, infinite intelligence, immune to retaining discord in thought. We can obey the demands of God. And the demands of God are that we be conscious of present harmony and perfection instead of an inharmonious past.

Hear these immortal words of the wise man: "That which hath been is now; and that which is to be hath already been; and God requireth that which is past." Since God requires the past, let us give it to Him. We do this by acknowledging that He has always controlled every iota of it, and that error has not done what it claims. There has never been a moment when we have not been God's perfect ideas. There has never been a moment when we have not known God as He is and our perfect selfhood as He has created it.

Then there is the reaction of irritation over what others say about us. The remedy is to know that there is one Mind, which understands and approves of us, and that therefore we cannot be misunderstood. And the remedy for resenting unpleasant situations is to know that God governs and that good is unfolding despite appearances. An irritated reaction to an unpleasant situation does not lessen or heal it — it merely shows that the error is still real to us. Why is it we are so disturbed when little things do not go our way? It is often a phase of egotism, which is being brought to the surface and deflated at occurrences to which we thought ourselves immune.

If we drop, break, or lose something, mortal mind has merely changed its sense testimony, but it cannot affect us. Incidents in the home or on the job that appear annoying are evil suggestions and would hide our spiritual selfhood derived from God, and hinder our demonstrating it. When we have removed friction-inducing errors from thought, our bodies and our experiences are certain to be harmonious. Even while we are working out our salvation here, our birthright is peace, poise, and balance. We do not need to wait until we have demonstrated perfection here to enjoy those qualities.

How do we react when someone rebukes or corrects us? We shall progress by following Mrs. Eddy's example in this regard. She writes: "If a friend informs us of a fault, do we listen patiently to the rebuke and credit what is said? Do we not rather give thanks that we are 'not as other men'? During many years the author has been most grateful for merited rebuke." (*Science and Health*)

Suppose we correct someone with a sincere desire to help, and the person whom we correct is resentful. What should be our attitude? Well, it is often wise in such instances not to argue, explain, or justify our part in the affair, but make certain in our own thought that no offense was intended, and to leave the result with God.

Then there is our reaction to failures or mistakes. This may be mortal mind's way of depressing us. To succumb to this phase of thought is to aid it in accomplishing its purpose. Of course we desire the correct understanding which turns a failure or mistake into a blessing. If we err in working out a problem, we do not contribute to its solution by condemning ourselves. We correct our errors. We learn what we can from the experience, then we are in a mental position to retain the lesson gained and not dwell further on the discord.

If we never attempt anything, we shall never err. But the goal of a Christian Scientist is not stagnation, nor yet the mere desire never to make a mistake. What is important is where our thought is spiritually. After all, it is always error that errs and fails. The fact is that only Truth is at work, exalting our thought above any sense of evil as personal or as real.

Again, reactions often stem from some emotion or strong feeling which disturbs or agitates. Suspicion, disgust, disappointment, greed, anger, fear, are emotional states. In the proportion that we know that only Truth and Love can motivate us do we demonstrate our immunity from reacting to these emotions. Certainly we do act, but always from the basis of healing what appears as a discordant bodily situation or human relationship. Our endeavor is to abide in a healing consciousness.

Actually, there is no reaction in Truth, in divine Love, and none in the consciousness of man, Love's likeness. The day must come, too, when we act only as Deity outlines. We can control not only our bodies, but also our affairs, through spiritually controlling our thought. In Science we exist in a state of dominion because we always have the dominion accorded man by Deity Himself. The only place we can exercise this dominion is in our consciousness. Nothing can prevent utilization of it. Nothing can prevent our experiencing the harmonious results which inevitably accompany our exercising it.

Through Christian Science we develop an understanding of the absolute unreality of evil. Enlightened and empowered by divine Mind, we think and act from the standpoint of our oneness, or unity, with God — from the standpoint of the continuous unfoldment of good and of nothing else. Keeping our thought imbued with the presence and control of Almighty God, we are certain to prove our dominion over every phase of reaction.

MAN "NEVER BELIEVES, BUT KNOWS"

A patient who had been ceaselessly voicing error sensed the resistance in the practitioner's thought. The patient's inquiry, "What are you thinking?" brought this response: "I don't believe a word you have been saying. You don't believe it either. Furthermore, you haven't really been saying it. It is a lie attempting to voice itself and deceive us both." This truth, made practical in Christian Science — that God's idea, man, does not believe evil and that error is no part of his consciousness, which is eternally a reflection of divine Mind — comforted this questioner just as it has many others.

We learn in Christian Science that God is infinite, all-knowing Mind. Writing on this point in *Science and Health*, Mrs. Eddy clearly states: "Spirit is the Ego which never dreams, but understands all things; which never errs, and is ever conscious; which never believes, but knows; which is never born and never dies. Spiritual man is the likeness of this Ego."

Since man is the likeness of Spirit, God, he "never believes, but knows." We cannot conceive of mortal mind's suggesting anything to God. Then it cannot suggest anything to God's likeness, man. Nor can it make him respond to its suggestion. As Mrs. Eddy says: "Matter cannot believe, and Mind understands. The body cannot believe. The believer and the belief are one and are mortal." (ibid).

Inasmuch as human thought is always externalized in what appear to be outward conditions and events, humanity's difficulties are induced by what it erroneously believes. Yet the ailment or discordant experience and the false belief which gives rise to it, are not two things, but one and the same — and that one is always to be handled as an erroneous belief. Our problems, then, are not something that we actually possess, but are merely incorrect suggestions we have believed or accepted. They are resolved when we realize that in our true selfhood we always know only spiritual facts and are immune to mesmeric suggestions. To the suggestions we can reply with these words of Jesus: "I never knew you: depart from me."

A student of Christian Science was praying to rise above a painful physical ailment. Although the condition seemed real, and although he seemed to believe it, he glimpsed the spiritual fact that not only was it untrue, but also he really did not believe it, because he understood his true selfhood to be harmonious. Seeing that it was no part of his consciousness as God's idea, he was able to reject the suggestion of pain with a sense of dominion that resulted in his complete release.

Error always remains in the realm of belief, for mortal mind's belief in evil does not get beyond itself — it cannot enter divine Mind or become attached to God's creation. Do we seem to be struggling with sickness? If so, we should reassure ourselves that only a false belief is arguing to our thought. The false belief will fade away as we fix our gaze on reality and awaken to our true selfhood. We shall perceive that the one perfect Mind always knows and does not erroneously believe. Man, in the likeness of this one Mind, is ever alert and clear. He is impervious to false beliefs. The believer and belief are not two, but as Mrs. Eddy tells us, "The believer and the belief are one and are mortal."

An erring belief in any phase of error is no part of divine Mind. Nor is man thinking, experiencing, or cognizing it, for the one all-knowing Mind, which is the Mind of everyone, is cognizant only of good. This being true, mankind can demonstrate over the undesirable traits that it encounters. Should someone appear to be greedy, we can know that man, in the image and likeness of God, does not desire to be and is not greedy, but expresses love and generosity. If we believe that man is greedy, an aggressive mental suggestion is attempting to make us accept greed as real and attach it to a person. The real man, understanding substance to be Spirit and knowing that he reflects infinite substance, is immune to any argument of greed.

If we seem to be the object of envy, we should realize that every step Spiritward, every demonstration of the capacities of divine Mind, is supported and blessed by our heavenly Father. God always protects every righteous effort of the one seeking Him. There is, in reality, no mortal mind to grudge maliciously or to be unwilling to recognize the expression of good. A businessman who was confronted with envy in his organization, learned that there is no envy in divine Mind and that consequently envy does not exist to use man, who reflects the one wholly good Mind. Conscious of the truth that every idea of God has all good, he proved his immunity to the suppositional darts of envy. These words of Jeremiah aptly describe aggressive suggestions and what is in store for them: "They are vanity, and the work of errors: in the time of their visitation they shall perish."

It is not to be inferred that Christian Scientists ignore evil in the form of sickness or sin. They humbly and honestly face what appear to be their own errors of thought and correct them. But they intelligently endeavor to correct them as powerless errors of belief, not as personal shortcomings or actual weaknesses. They strive earnestly to see the flawless selfhood of every individual as eternally at one with God, and as ever in heaven.

In his healing ministry Christ Jesus was not influenced by erring belief. Convinced of God's allness and of man's present perfection in His likeness, Jesus was governed by this positive conviction. Our Master knew that man is well. Consequently the unreal, evil suggestions, externalized as sickness or sin, could not exist in his enlightened consciousness. It is cause for great gratitude that Mrs. Eddy has revealed to humanity that sickness is no part of man's consciousness, but is a false, extraneous belief possessing no more reality than a dream!

Man ever lives, moves, and has his being in God, divine Mind, who is his source and substance. His true selfhood is spiritual and harmonious, hence unimpairable and indestructible. Being the likeness of his perfect Maker, man is never deceived by error, but is always conscious of good only, alert and ever awake to his radiant, spiritual selfhood. His intelligent consciousness cannot yield to error, for being the likeness of Spirit, the Ego which "understands all things," he never believes, but knows.

THE RIGHT QUESTION

Christian Science does not ignore evil but destroys it on the basis of its unreality and the omnipotence of God, infinite good. Humanity has wrestled unintelligently with sin and disease because it has accepted them as realities. Mrs. Eddy explains this important point in the Christian Science textbook, where she says: "Human hypotheses first assume the reality of sickness, sin, and death, and then assume the necessity of these evils because of their admitted actuality. These human verdicts are the procurers of all discord."

The question, "Where did evil come from?" has many diverse facets. One phase of it may cause an individual burdened with the belief in disease to wonder, "Why am I sick?" That is the wrong question. As Christian Scientists, we are not interested in ascertaining why we are ill. We really wish to understand the reality of our being, our present perfection as God's spiritual ideas. Our desire is to demonstrate that God, good, is ever present, and that this dream of mortal existence has no reality.

Someone, evidently troubled because of evil's seeming reality, asked Mrs. Eddy, "If God made all that was made, and it was good, where did evil originate?" And she clearly answers in part: "It never originated or existed as an entity. It is but a false belief, even the belief that God is not what the Scriptures imply Him to be, All-in-all, but that there is an opposite intelligence or mind termed evil." (*Miscellaneous Writings*) And, she adds: "The leading self-evident proposition of Christian Science is: good being real, evil, good's opposite, is unreal. This truism needs only to be tested scientifically to be found true, and adapted to destroy the appearance of evil to an extent beyond the power of any doctrine previously entertained." (ibid)

Thus we see that in Christian Science the basis of our reasoning must always be the reality of good and the nothingness of evil. Indeed, the unreality of evil may be likened to a dream. A dream does not affect one. No matter how vicious a nightmare is, it is ended when the dreamer awakes. A loud alarm usually puts an end to any nightmare. Science reveals the Christ as here, breaking the belief, or dream, of error. The Christ comes to human consciousness, and so awakens and enlightens it that it can no longer go on dreaming, believing in error.

The wrong question is, "How did I happen to dream?" The right question, the one that concerns us, is "How can I learn that I have always been awake to reality?" Mrs. Eddy gives us the proper method: "Reasoning from cause to effect in the Science of Mind, we begin with Mind, which must be understood through the idea which expresses it and cannot be learned from its opposite, matter. Thus we arrive at Truth, or intelligence, which evolves its own unerring idea and never can be coordinate with human illusions." (*Science and Health*)

So in Christian Science we begin with God, with perfect cause, and we reason, not from sense testimony back to cause, but from cause to effect. We admit the facts of divine Science, which are clear to divine intelligence or spiritual sense. We are governed by spiritual sense, by what we know. Holding to what we know, we contradict what we see, and the real and true, which has always been present and which sense testimony has been attempting to hide, appears to our enlightened thought.

In many situations humanity is governed by what it knows. The experienced sea captain is undisturbed by what to his frightened passengers may seem to be a serious storm. It is serious to them, but not to him. His knowledge of his ship and of the weather and his nautical experience preclude the entrance of doubt or fear. The trained auto mechanic is undismayed when an excited individual cannot start his car. His mechanical knowledge and experience usually enable him to rectify quickly the apparent trouble. Similar instances from business and daily life are legion.

And what of the sick one before us? Reflecting the intelligence of God, we know that all that is present is a harmonious, orderly expression of divine Mind. Jesus' thought was so clearly a reflection of Mind that he beheld, not the discordant picture before him, but the perfect man of God, the man he knew to be present. The correct view, Science explains, heals the sick. And it does so because sickness is not in man, but in an erring view of him. Because we have dominion over our own thinking, we have power to deal with all that presents itself to us. Beginning with God, Mind, enables us to rise spiritually until that which before seemed real becomes unreal to our enlightened thought. As we go on living and demonstrating the truth, we shall see more and more clearly that good alone has presence and the evil is never present.

Because evil is illusory, it can never become true or existent, nor can it affect one's real being. We do not ignore evil or continue to indulge it. Instead, we humbly correct it and turn from it, praying as did Job: "That which I see not teach thou me: if I have done iniquity, I will do no more." Moreover, as we live spiritually and learn to discipline our thinking, we are able to recognize the various phases of suppositional animal magnetism, or evil mind, and to handle them specifically. We definitely resist evil at every point and refute all its arguments. The beginning of this intelligent resistance is indeed the beginning of victory.

A subtle error which would hinder our demonstrations of Christian Science is the attempt of animal magnetism to have us first accept as real what appears as a personal problem, and then have us work to get rid of it. What appears as our problem or difficulty is to be recognized as a phase of impersonal evil, the mortal dream. Our responsibility is to know Truth. It is the nature of Truth to destroy error and make free. So we do more than refrain from attempting to account for evil — we refuse to acquiesce in its mesmeric suggestions. We see through them to the spiritual facts they are attempting to hide. The practical application of these fundamental truths is of vital importance.

Suppose the question should present itself, "How did I ever get so involved?" Obviously, that is the wrong question. The truth is that man is not a mortal in a trying situation. The difficulty has not touched man or become part of his experience. One's true self-hood, abiding in God and immune to evil suggestion, is what one is most interested in discerning and demonstrating. Perhaps we hear: "What is wrong with me? How did I ever make such a mistake?" Such questions arise because we have accepted sense testimony. Naturally, we are desirous of avoiding past errors. As we turn to omniscient Mind, our Mind, this Mind uncovers as unreal any error we may need to destroy. Denying it and obliterating it from consciousness, we shall have the evidence of its nothingness.

The right question is, "How can I apprehend and demonstrate my glorious spiritual selfhood which is ever at one with infallible, unerring Truth?" Isaiah gives a telling answer: "Ask me of things to come concerning my sons, and concerning the work of my hands command ye me." Here is God's invitation to call on Him with assurance while we claim our present perfection — "the work of His hands."

Another wrong question is, "Why did this happen to me?" We are not to admit error's false claim to have overthrown God's harmonious government. The right question is, "How can I see that God's law of harmony has always been operating and that He has been governing every moment?"

It is evil that would have us start our thinking at some point of error, accounting for it, analyzing it, being disappointed over it, feeling frustrated because of it, or resenting it. The important point regarding animal magnetism is that it is unreal, powerless, and has never done what it claims. And our interest is always in admitting and demonstrating its nothingness through perceiving and acknowledging the presence and power of God, good.

Wrong questions should be unmasked. They represent the voice of the enemy, evil's attempt to have us admit its false claims and argue on its side. This is animal magnetism's method of having us work against and defeat our demonstrations of Science. Paul's words are true: "We know that all things work together for good to them that love God, to them who are the called according to his purpose." The apostle does not say that some things work together for good, but that "all things work together for good to them that love God." The fact is that God, Truth, alone is operating and that error is always defeated. Because of the activity of Truth, error may be more in evidence due to its being brought to the surface while being destroyed. Yet the law of God is a law of the uninterrupted unfoldment of good, and each moment the child of divine Love is being blessed.

Our Leader saw this clearly. When maligned and persecuted, she did not attempt with human means to halt the unjust attacks. She knew that when they no longer blessed they would cease; so she alertly claimed and demonstrated the blessing that was hers in what seemed to be an untoward experience.

"All things work together for good to them that love God." Everything that comes to us can bless us if we realize that in reality we have not been and cannot be separated from our God, ever-present, infinite good. The law is that God governs and that good is unfolding despite appearances. As we accept this law for our government, we shall become a law unto ourselves that evil cannot harm us. We shall prove in increasing measure that God's law of the certain, unopposable unfoldment of good is operative at all times and in all places.

In our experience we shall cease to attempt to account for evil, cease to admit its mesmeric claims, cease to be a mouthpiece for error, inquiring what is wrong or limited or discordant. On the contrary, we shall work more and more positively until we ask the right question that applies in each instance, and basically it will be much like this: "How can I understand and accept what is true now — God's all-inclusive perfection — and demonstrate my radiant spiritual selfhood in His likeness?" And asking it with earnestness and sincerity, we cannot fail to receive the right answer.

"WHAT AM I?"

In two lines Matthew Arnold gives this terse formula for overcoming trouble:

> *Resolve to be thyself; and know, that he*
> *Who finds himself, loses his misery.*

The understanding that one can lose all misery through finding himself, furnishes one with a great incentive to comprehend what he really is. Under the marginal heading, "The armor of divinity," Mary Baker Eddy writes in *Science and Health*, "Know thyself, and God will supply the wisdom and the occasion for a victory over evil." Let us consider how a true knowledge of oneself gained through the teachings of Christian Science solves our problems.

The average individual classifies himself according to his business or profession. Then, unless he is alert, he will tend to take on the prevailing beliefs and limitations associated with his occupation. For example, if one is an actor, he may feel that he is subject to seasonal employment. A musician may unconsciously exhibit the temperamental traits attributed to those of his profession. A salesman or an advertising manager may find himself undergoing the tension common to his fellow workers.

A businessman was under a great sense of pressure. "Do you think of yourself as a sales manager?" queried a Christian Science practitioner. "Certainly," came the rejoinder, "that's what I am." The practitioner then made clear that irrespective of how highly esteemed one's present occupation may be, to regard oneself as in a certain business is limitation. "Your real and only business," continued the practitioner, "is to be man, to show forth the intelligence and attributes of your Maker. A sales managership is merely a temporal activity wherein you are afforded the opportunity to express God and your true selfhood." This changed the thought of the sales manager. Going to his position as man, who is endowed with infinite intelligence by his Maker, and hence possesses the answer to every problem, brought release from a false sense of responsibility.

Demonstrating one's activity as God's man brings to one's vocation all the qualities of God. Then, if duties seem burdensome, one needs to enlarge his thinking, to come into a better understanding of what he actually is. He gains this from looking not to a material occupation to determine his status, but to his source, God. The prophet Isaiah admonishes: "Hearken to me, ye that seek the Lord: look unto the rock whence ye are hewn, and to the hole of the pit whence ye are digged."

Even humanly speaking, one is not in a certain business. On the contrary, his business is included in his thinking. How and why? One's entire activity, being embraced in his thought, will be stagnant or progressive according to the thoughts he impresses upon it. His occupation or business cannot think for him, therefore, it cannot control him. But because he includes his business in his thinking, and because he has dominion over his own thought, he has dominion over his business.

Man is not a mortal, subject to the demands of a material activity, limited by its prospects and possessed by an occupation or an employer. He eternally belongs to God. As Isaiah declared: "Now thus saith the Lord that created thee, O Jacob, and he that formed thee, O Israel, Fear not: for I have redeemed thee, I have called thee by thy name; thou art mine." So man is a spiritual idea, having limitless intelligence and opportunity, for whom good is unfolding in accord with God's unopposable spiritual law.

We cannot conceive of man, God's likeness, as needing anything. Being the perfect reflection of all-inclusive Being, man must include the right concept of home, church, and activity. Because God is his Shepherd, he lacks nothing. Therefore, he is not in the business of getting, but must be in the business of expressing all the qualities of God. And that is the real man's eternal, enriching, satisfying employment.

Because man is one with God in intelligence and action, he has no volition of his own, but reflects the one divine volition. He cannot be separated from God and His goodness. Reflection cannot cease or be stopped, but must always image forth the harmonious activity of infinite Spirit. In the words of our great Master: "The Son can do nothing of himself, but what he seeth the Father do: for what things soever he doeth, these also doeth the Son likewise."

God's perfection must be man's as His expression. God would always declare, "I can because I AM," never, "I can't." But man is the son of I AM, or God. Man can therefore say, "I (man) can because God is." Indeed, man represents God's allness and ability.

In Christian Science, one does not work from the standpoint that what he needs is available, but outside of him to be acquired, but from the standpoint that, as man, he already includes all good. Accordingly, one strives less to heal some discord which appears real to him, and more to be conscious of the present perfection of man. He resists the aggressive suggestions of animal magnetism, which would cause him to doubt his all-inclusiveness and present perfection, and admits both with no mental reservation. As our Leader tells us: "The admission to one's self that man is God's own likeness sets man free to master the infinite idea." (*Science and Health*)

To understand truly what one is, involves seeing oneself not as a mortal, but as a spiritual idea. But if one believes others to be defective and discordant, he cannot say in truth, "I understand what I am." One does not really comprehend his own perfect selfhood if he believes in imperfection in others. So it is essential that we should see everyone as actually a perfect child of God.

To be clear as to one's true selfhood is to see also man's pre-existence and eternal oneness with God as His idea. This eradicates the belief in an unhappy material past. Since man is the perpetual expression of God, he is not, and never has been, a medium of lack, loneliness, or disease. There is no mortal mind to rehearse a so-called discordant or evil experience. Man has not been in such an experience, for he has always thought, felt, and acted in accord with the perfect law of God.

Do you falsely take pride in feeling that you are self-made? To be self-made would be impossible, for God created man. Man really possesses nothing of his own. All belongs to God. As reflection, man understands, and hence possesses, the affluence and attributes of Deity. Then, too, to feel that you, instead of God, are father or mother, may involve a false sense of burden and responsibility, which forfeits the joy and freedom that stem from acknowledging God as Father and Mother. There is one creator, one Father-Mother, even God. There is one family of spiritual ideas, created, supplied, and held in perfection by Him.

If a woman believes she is one of the so-called weaker sex, she should change her thought and acknowledge that she is complete in Science, strong at all points. Then she is in a mental position to free herself from false physiological laws. She will also prove her freedom from unfair compensation and unjust business practices based upon a wrong sense of womanhood.

If one has a sense of superiority because of certain illustrious forebears, or a sense of inferiority because of less worthy ancestors, he is believing in heredity and may come under its false laws. But in neither case, can one be affected if he acknowledges his incorruptible inheritance as the son of God. To say, "She looks older for her age than I do for mine," is to believe in age, with the possibility of experiencing its effects, for thus one fails to comprehend man's eternal, unimpairable existence as Mind's spiritual idea. He believes, instead, that evil is real and personal. The scientific way is to see everyone as a spiritual child of God, reflecting Deity's inexhaustible qualities and faculties.

Healings have come to individuals who have refused to be

limited by a past, by an occupation, or by a physical problem. What mortal mind suggests as our present problem is not important. What God knows about us is the one important point. Listening for and accepting His voice, we shall recognize and find ourselves rejoicing in what we are, the children of God, untouched by anything that mortal mind may suggest.

Mrs. Eddy writes in *The First Church of Christ, Scientist and Miscellany:* "As an active portion of one stupendous whole, goodness identifies man with universal good. Thus may each member of this church rise above the oft-repeated inquiry, What am I? to the scientific response: I am able to impart truth, health, and happiness, and this is my rock of salvation and my reason for existing." In this reference our Leader clearly indicates what the spiritualized individual is able to do and his "reason for existing." This she terms the scientific response to the question, "What am I?"

It is heartening to know that we do not need to improve God's creation; we need only to understand what He has already done. This results in a more harmonious manifestation right here. Man has no material history that can perpetuate a lie, no present problem that can hide from him what he is — the emanation of Deity Himself. Nor can anything obscure from those who understand this fact their "reason for existing" — their ability "to impart truth, health, and happiness."

Man has no alternative but to express God, to be the glorious reflection of the Almighty. To accept joyously this divine right, to live the Christ, to express unselfish love, is to glimpse now what it means to be man, the blessed child of God. Then shall we most assuredly have gained a satisfying answer to the question, "What am I?"

ACCEPTING THE TRUE REPORT

The story of Jonah has typified to many the experience of mortals when evil seems to beset them on every side, and there is no apparent means of deliverance. The narrative records: "The waters compassed me about, even to the soul: the depth closed me round about, the weeds were wrapped about my head." Yet there must have come to Jonah in some measure the conviction that his seemingly hopeless experience was not so much an external condition from which he needed deliverance, as an erroneous thought condition which needed correction, for his memorable prayer wholeheartedly acknowledged God and His power to deliver: "When my soul fainted within me I remembered the Lord: and my prayer came in unto thee, into thine holy temple. They that observe lying vanities forsake their own mercy. But I will sacrifice unto thee with the voice of thanksgiving; I will pay that that I have vowed. Salvation is of the Lord."

It is only material sense that faints — becomes downcast. At the very moment it aggressively argues defeat, we, like Jonah, can remember God's power and lift our prayers to Him by whom they are always heard. We, too, can give up the false beliefs of defeat, discouragement, hopelessness and so on, and sacrifice the belief that these qualities are real. We can vision the present unimpaired safety and perfection of God's spiritual idea, which error cannot obscure, and refuse to forsake our "own mercy" by not observing or acquiescing in its false arguments. Having taken our stand determinedly, we shall have the evidence that "salvation is of the Lord." We can see and accept, not what error says cannot be done, but what God says He has already done, and what man as His reflection is expressing now. Nothing can hinder our healing ourselves of accepting discouraging adverse reports.

We have but to listen to God's angel message, revealing ever-present spiritual facts. "There is no speech nor language, where their voice is not heard," sang the Psalmist. There is no time or place where His voice, the utterance of Love that destroys fear, and of Truth that eliminates falsity, is not heard. In every human situation, the Christ, Truth, is present with its redeeming message. The spiritual fact or true report about home, body, business, or supply is eternally at hand to accept. Christian Scientists should strive for and accomplish quick healings. It is gratifying to see rapid and constant improvement as the result of faithful work. But if, in spite of the truth declared, progress seems delayed, the healing work is going on although symptoms may not indicate it. A student of Christian Science had been struggling for several days with a painful disorder, including fever and weakness. The symptoms and discomfort seemed very real to him. That evening he promised to acknowledge the facts of his spiritual, harmonious being. Although the symptoms had worsened, he told the practitioner that he was not accepting them, that he had made definite spiritual progress, and that he was now controlling his thinking and felt confident about the demonstration. His intuition proved correct, for later that night the improvement was marked, and the following day he was able to arise and go to his office.

Christian Science reveals that what mortal mind terms a business problem or a discordant bodily condition is entirely mental, a phase of ignorant human belief objectified. As it becomes clear that we are not dealing with a real condition that is to be changed, but only with an erroneous thought — a false report that needs to be corrected and replaced with the spiritual fact — one will not be afraid or doubt. What appears real seems so to erring belief. It is not a reality to man in God's likenes,s and has never been real at all. When patients appear sick, the sickness is not an actuality. Their real need is to be healed of the belief that the real man is or can be sick. It is helpful for one to drop all thought of himself as a mortal needing healing. Really, the need is for improvement of thought —

the changing of consciousness from a material to a spiritual basis. Progress is judged not by what matter presents, but by what one cognizes and demonstrates of his true, unblemished selfhood in the likeness of Spirit. Our Leader asks: "Who remembers that patience, forgiveness, abiding faith, and affection, are the symptoms by which our Father indicates the different stages of man's recovery from sin and his entrance into Science?" *(Miscellaneous Writings)*

Thought illumined by God is never darkened or confused by false reports about man's present perfect selfhood. Mortal mind's assumption that God's idea is accepting and responding to its beliefs is utterly false. In *Science* and *Health* Mrs. Eddy writes: "According to Christian Science, the only real senses of man are spiritual, emanating from divine Mind. Thought passes from God to man, but neither sensation nor report goes from material body to Mind. The intercommunication is always from God to His idea, man."

Animal magnetism can make no report to the real man. When mortal mind reports symptoms of disease, failure, lack, and separation from God, it is not a report of a status that exists. It is a false claim that has never appeared to the divine Mind or to Mind's intelligent idea, man, who eternally cognizes reality. It seems real only because we give reality to the unreal. If the physical senses tell us what is true, Jesus would have been wrong in overcoming their testimony. He never acquiesced in their false report, but refuted it with the true report of man's perfection, which he ever listened for and received from the Father.

The multiplication of false reports does not make them true, any more than a million people believing five plus five equals eleven would make it so. No amount of false believing can ever alter one figure in mathematics. Similarly, disease being unreal, there is never a moment when mesmerism can bring it into being. Credence can give it only seeming reality. Nor will time correct a mistake or a false report. Time will not eliminate a bookkeeper's error if he puts his books away for ten years. Intelligence alone will solve it in either instance. Similarly, a problem of continued lack, or a chronic disease, is no more difficult because it claims duration.

The Christian Science practitioner does not believe a false report arguing persistency, disease, or lack of improvement. The report, being false, is not known to man, nor is it circulating in God's universe. The practitioner accepts as true the report which divine Mind imparts. He abides in the consciousness of the allness of God, and is not influenced by the false reports of mortal mind. Irrespective of the claim, he continues to trust the spiritual facts that have been revealed to him by God.

Isaiah wrote: "I, even I, am he that blotteth out thy transgressions for mine own sake, and will not remember thy sins. Put me in remembrance: let us plead together: declare thou, that thou mayest be justified." When the truth of man's glorious being is accepted, it will so illumine consciousness as to blot out any sense of transgression or incapacity as part of one's experience. God does not associate sin and sickness with His offspring. Human thought can remember or know nothing about man, the unsullied purity, the undepleted health and uninvadable perfection that are inherent in his being as a child of God. Those who declare and live with the healing, transforming truths that Love eternally imparts will "be justified," and will have the evidence of them.

The real man is undeviatingly perfect. His consciousness includes only right ideas — hence it does not include any wrong concept of body, health, supply, or success. In it there is no unyielding erroneous belief, nothing that desires to or can resist the truth. Man has no capacity derived from God wherewith to respond to mortal mind's reports of sin or sickness, or to express them. He knows good alone.

God's pure thoughts, His angels, pass directly to man, who is at one with God. They alone eternally impel, inspire, and control him. They make clear his true, Godlike nature as impervious to evil beliefs. They reveal his health as unassailable, his every function and action as spiritual and harmonious. They counteract every suggestion of obstruction and discord with the understanding that man includes the true sense of action as free and harmonious because God-governed. They ever enlighten and acquaint one with his limitless supply and fresh opportunities.

After He had given him the Ten Commandments, "the Lord said unto Moses, Thus thou shalt say unto the children of Israel, Ye have seen that I have talked with you from Heaven." Listening to God's voice enables us to deal with difficult situations from the standpoint of present harmony and perfection. The Scriptures further state: "In all places where I record my name I will come unto thee, and I will bless thee." In every quiet sanctuary of thought, whenever to consciousness God's perfect nature and man in His likeness are revealed, God's presence will be a reality to us, will come unto us and will bless us.

We should continually claim the right report from heaven. Mortal mind's report cannot alter one iota of reality, but the voice from heaven and harmony accepted, silences mortal mind's report and replaces it with the spiritual fact. Let us be grateful that in the Science of Christianity revelation and demonstration are one. We can rest in the assurance that the angel thoughts which reveal man's perfection enable us to demonstrate it, for in the words of a hymn:

The thought of Thee is mightier far
Than sin and pain and sorrow are.

For further information regarding Christian Science:
Write: The Bookmark
         Post Office Box 801143
         Santa Clarita, CA 91380
Call: 1-800-220-7767
Visit our website: www. thebookmark.com

Sunshine

Sunshine

A Novel by

Norma Klein

Sunshine is based on the television production
written by Carol Sobieski, suggested by the Journal
of Jacquelyn M. Helton.
Originated by Lawrence Schiller, an Alskog, Inc.
book in association with the Jennifer Elizabeth
Helton Trust.

Holt, Rinehart and Winston
New York

Published simultaneously in Canada by Holt, Rinehart and
Winston of Canada, Limited
Published by arrangement with Avon Books.

Library of Congress Cataloging in Publication Data

Klein, Norma, 1938–
  Sunshine

  I. Title.
PZ4.K643Su3 [PS3561.L35]   813'.5'4   75-10787
ISBN 0-03-015196-1

Printed in the United States of America

10 9 8 7 6 5 4 3 2

To Arthur Root

A young woman, Jacquelyn M. Helton, died in 1971 of a rare form of cancer, osteogenic sarcoma. The last eighteen months of her life she kept a tape-recorded diary as a legacy for her young daughter. Norma Klein's novel has been written from the actual diary and from Carol Sobieski's script of the television motion picture that appeared in 1973.

Part One

It's funny how you can tell when people are lying to you. Not lying, really, that's not what I mean, I guess. But this doctor, Dr. Thompson—God, I've gone to him four times with this lump on my leg and each time he has some other story. First it was the baby. Jill's six months old now and my figure is pretty much back to normal. I'm skinny usually, but when I had her I did gain a lot of weight. Too much. So he said it was that. He claimed somehow being too fat put a strain on me since this apartment Sam and I are living in has two flights of stairs. He said carrying the baby plus being too fat was what did it.

It's not that. Even I know that. There's only two flights of stairs and Jill's not that heavy. I mean, now she is, but she wasn't back then when he said it. I just get the feeling he doesn't know what's wrong so he makes

3

all this stuff up. Just say you don't know, I want to tell him.

Then, the other time it was the cold climate. Well, it's cold, sure, but our place is warm enough. No, he said the cold was in my joints and was making me stiff. You just wait till it gets warm, he says. Okay, I'll wait. There's not much else to do, is there? Only the shots he gives me hurt and I don't think they're helping. My leg still hurts. It's silly, I guess, I still hate shots so much. I always did as a kid too. At school they used to make us line up to get our shots and what was worst was the fact that we couldn't go off in a little room and bawl and scream our eyes out. No, we had to stand there right in front of all our friends, with them watching. I hated it!

I've got bursitis, that's what he says. Like arthritis, sort of. But that's something old people get! My Aunt May, she had bursitis, but she was, like, sixty something. I'm nineteen. Oh, he doesn't know what he's saying. The trouble is, this town we're in, well, there aren't so many doctors and I didn't want to go to some real expensive one. Where would we get the money? I don't get any alimony from David, I don't want to, either, and Sam—well, he did save some money from the last couple of years when he had all these odd jobs, you know, working at gas stations and stuff. But now, he doesn't want to do that anymore. He wants to try and get a job playing the guitar. That's his real love—country western music. And he's good, he's really great. I know he'll make it, if he can have a chance.

When I get home, there's Sam sitting on the bed with Weaver. They're practicing their music. I love watching Sam when he plays. He gets this kind of thoughtful

4

tender expression—you can tell just by his face how much he loves it. Weaver—well, he's something else. He's my cousin, and I don't like him that much. He's just kind of sarcastic, the kind who always makes you feel like you've done or said something stupid. That's what Weaver's like. I know he thinks that because of me, Sam doesn't have enough time to practice, that his whole heart and soul isn't in his music. That's not even true, really, but even if it were—love's important too, isn't it? You can't play music all day long. Weaver thinks I'm jealous. I'm not, that's not fair. I have my puss, my little darling, Jill; they can have their darn music.

Whew, Jill's getting kind of heavy, the old, fat puss face. I get her out of the backyard and start taking off her snowsuit. I love babies in snowsuits with just their round faces with these red, red cheeks peeking out. Like Eskimo babies.

"Hey, that sounds good," I call over to them. "Remind me to hire you when I get rich."

Weaver just goes on playing like I wasn't there. To Sam he says, "The bridges still need work."

Oh get a girl, Weaver! Know what it's like to be young and in love, you dumbhead! I guess I ought to feel sorry for him. If he weren't so nasty to me, maybe I would.

I go into the kitchen to open some chili for supper. We've been eating simply—chili, hamburgers. I don't mind it. I mean, I like good food too, but this is okay. We have everything else—so we don't have steak. Sometimes I think that if we had everything, that would be too much. We have so much more than most people,

5

anyway. Than most people ever have. I know that, partly I guess, because I was married once and it wasn't good, so I know what good is. I think a lot of people never know. A lot of girls might have stayed with David and thought that was what life was all about, wouldn't ever expect to get more. But I knew there was more. Just kind of by instinct, I knew. I think you have to trust your instinct about those things.

"What was the verdict, baby?" Sam calls in.

"Oh, same old stuff . . . bursitis."

"What'd he give you for it?"

"A shot . . . it hurt."

"I thought last time he gave you a shot and it didn't do any good."

"Yeah, well, this time he says it will do good . . . I can try out for the Olympic track team tomorrow."

"Does this guy know what he's doing?" Sam says. "He keeps giving you these shots—"

I smile. I love teasing Sam. "Well, if you have to know, we're having this thing, see, and we figured you'd never find out if I had to keep going back for my knee."

With a big roar, Sam leaps up from the bed, runs into the kitchen and starts kissing me, hugging me, laughing. He's big and his face scratches. Wow, I love him, he's like a bear.

He makes a sign to Weaver to leave, and Weaver gets this real sour look. "You oughta be a plumber, man, not a musician," he says.

But he leaves. Good riddance, old pal. We roll on the bed, kissing and hugging. Jill is looking at us, puzzled, not knowing what's going on. Sam lifts her up and brings her down on the bed with us. I feel like everything I love is in this bed with me right now, my baby, my guy, and we're all rolled up in the quilt, laughing. Once I saw this statue of a man and a woman and a child but they were all one, all carved together, and that's how I feel when we're all together like this. We're one thing, one person.

I used to think it would matter that Sam wasn't Jill's father. I mean, I thought he couldn't love her the way a real father could. But it's not so. He's so good to her, so patient, so kind. Now he says he would've gone with me just for her, only when we met, she wasn't even born yet. But she was in me, she was part of me. I feel Sam never knew me before Jill. He's always known me happy. I guess if he'd met me when I was with David, he wouldn't have thought much of me. I was always in a rotten mood then, always complaining. Now I feel I had a right to be. I mean, I think people deserve to be happy, and if they're not they have a right to feel cheated. Of course, who said I had to marry him, at sixteen especially? Yeah, I realize that. It was my choice and sort of a dumb one. I wanted to get away from home mostly, that was the main part.

And David's not a monster. He's—well, he's much straighter than Sam. He went through college and he was already studying to be a geologist when I met him. He seemed so grown-up to me. All the kids I knew didn't know which end was up. Maybe that was from living in a small town—Three Forks—but also they were young. The guys I knew were so young, they didn't know anything. David seemed so solid. I was really flattered when he noticed me. And he'd listen when I talked—I was a real chatterbox then. He'd listen, like

7

what I said was important and smart. He wasn't a monster, David. I guess now that I have Sam I don't resent David so much. I feel like maybe someday he'll meet the right girl and be happy, only I wasn't the right girl. He'd never have been happy with me. He said he was. He said he never could see what I was complaining about, but I think he did see, he just didn't want to admit it. He's one of those slow, cautious people who decides things slowly, but when he does he hates to admit he was wrong.

You might find it hard to believe this, but David wouldn't even sleep with me before we got married. He thought I was too young, what would my parents say. He's like that—honorable. We had these crazy scenes where I'd be saying—oh let's, why not, we're engaged and all that, and he'd say no, we ought to wait. I guess I liked that in him too, though it seemed a little crazy. I mean, most other guys always seemed to want to, whether they loved you or not, and he really did love me and he wanted to wait. I dug that, I really did.

The thing that got me so mad, more than mad, hurt really, was when I told Mom we were getting married and she said, "You little whore." She was sure I was pregnant! I wasn't! Gosh, I was a virgin, even, and one reason I was was because she'd been screaming at us—there were four of us, all girls—ever since I can remember about how important it was to be a virgin when you got married. And I wanted to please her. I was like a little girl, in that way. Well, I *was* a little girl—just sixteen. Not that eighteen's so old, but now, having been married and with Jill—I feel so much older. Much more than just two and a half years older. Then, I had been living at home all my life, except for this one summer when I ran away, when I was fourteen. And when Mom said that, I just felt so awful. I'd done exactly what she said we should do and it didn't matter, she still didn't trust me or love me. Why?

It's so crazy, but Mom has never really loved me. And I feel like I must have done something bad to make her feel that way. I'd almost rather think it was because I did something bad than to think it just happened, for no good reason. Partly, which is funny, I think I remind her of herself. I look like her, more than the others do. I have long black hair like hers and hell, I'm pretty. I was always "the pretty one," but pretty like her, kind of sassy and smart. And I think I was like her in being kind of emotional and saying and doing what I felt. Winona —she's my oldest sister—she's kind of calm and solid, more like Dad's side of the family. She's not married, she lives in New York now and she's studying biology. I loved her the most because she was like a mommy to me, very kind and gentle. Whenever Mom or Dad were mean to me, I'd go to Winona. She didn't always take my side, but she was kind. Even though we were so different. And she loves the land, like me—that was another bond between us, especially as I got older. I guess Mom respected Winona, even though they weren't that close. Winona was so smart, Mom was always a little scared of her.

Darleen is the next one, two years younger than Winona. She's married now with four kids and she lives right near Mom and Dad. Her husband, Joe, works in a hardware store. For some reason, Mom and Darleen always got on like crazy. Almost like two friends at school, whispering and hugging. I felt so left out when they were together. Even now that Darleen is married, she comes to Mom for everything and I mean everything! Mom even goes over there and sets Darleen's hair and helps her tint it this revolting yellow color every week. And they trade recipes; they're into that whole housewife bit. I really wonder sometimes what would happen to Darleen if Mom died or even moved away, not that that's likely in the immediate future. But I think she might just flip out. I guess that makes Mom feel good, feeling so needed. I mean, I needed her too, but I could never show it the same way. If I know someone loves me, like with Sam, I can show it, but I hate that feeling of pleading with someone for love, it's too demeaning.

Pat is the baby, she's younger than me. Maybe I was sort of the middle child. I think Mom had Darleen and Winona and then might have stopped, but Dad really wanted a boy so they figured they'd keep trying. I think that's stupid. I'd never, *never* have a baby if I wasn't going to love it no matter what. And I wouldn't care what my husband or anyone said. So then I came along and I guess everyone was real disappointed. And I was one of those wriggly, fresh little kids that gets into everything and messes things up—Winona and Darleen were really neat, both of them. So maybe I wasn't such a joy to have around. By the time Pat came, I think Mom didn't care so much. I think she knew she wasn't going to have a boy and was sort of reconciled to it. Pat is little and thin and pale—she's always had some kind of sickness since she was born. Starting when she was three, she had to wear these glasses; her eyes are really bad,

10

she's almost blind without them. So she was everyone's baby. I love her a lot. I guess I was mean to her when we were little. I didn't want her tagging around after me, and I always made her be the dog or the baby in our games, but I love her. I felt like I wanted to take care of her and be good to her—she's like that.

I don't like the nighttime. It seems like at night all the bad things that happened during the day, all the things I've worried about but pushed away, come creeping back. Not always, just sometimes. This one night I fell asleep and had a nightmare. It was all mixed up, not really clear—my dreams never are—but in it the doctor was telling me something bad about my leg, that I was going to die, and I woke up so scared. It was so real!

Sam is sleeping—he always sleeps like a log. Jill is in her crib, sleeping too. I hate waking Sam up, it doesn't seem fair. But I feel so lonely and scared sitting here, being the only one awake.

Finally, I give him just a little shove and whisper, "Sam?"

He opens his eyes and holds me in his arms, the way I

12

want him to. Oh, I feel better, but worse, too. I'm crying, I knew I would. "He's wrong, Sam," I say. "That doctor . . . it's something worse . . . I know."

He strokes my head. "Sweetheart . . . don't."

It's so good to be here with him. "Ssh," he says. "Don't wake Jill . . ."

"But I had this dream," I say.

"Dreams don't mean anything."

I want him to be right. Oh, I know, if you asked me in the morning, do dreams mean anything, I'd say no, of course not, don't be silly. But now—it seemed so real. I can almost remember the doctor's face.

Sam goes back to sleep with his arms still around me. He's so loving, so good. Am I too happy? Oh, that's silly, that's superstitious again. I remember when I was little and scared of the dark, I used to go into Mom and Dad's room. They didn't like me to, so I wouldn't even tell them I was there. I'd just creep into their bed at the foot of it and stay there till I felt better. Only once I fell asleep and wet the bed and Dad woke up and got really mad at me.

Jill, I won't do that to you. I'll let you come in my bed whenever you want. I don't care if you wet it. You're scared, that's all, and when babies are scared, they wet their pants. I hate the way Darleen is with her children—just the way Mom was with us, I guess, too strict and setting dumb rules that don't even make sense. I want Jill to be free, the way I wasn't.

She's such a good baby. I miss having her wake up at night and want to nurse. When she was six weeks, she slept right through the night! Such an angel! Just by herself she did it. But I used to like getting up and

13

nursing her. It would be so quiet and I'd bring her into bed with me. I'd prop myself up with a pillow and she'd drink quietly, and Sam would be sleeping there. I never felt scared then, even though it was dark. I just felt really peaceful and good.

I always wanted a baby, especially a baby girl, but I always wondered too if it would be as good as they say. So many things aren't. So many things they build up in this false romantic way that I hate. So I wondered if maybe having a baby wouldn't be like that. But it was great. Not just having her but nursing her, holding her. I want to nurse her till she's a year. I guess when her teeth start coming in, it might hurt a little, but her teeth aren't in yet, they're slow, I guess. Good. Let them be slow.

Wake up, Jill, wake up and comfort me. Let me hold you. No, I can't wake her up just to comfort me, that's selfish. I just look over at her. She sleeps on her stomach. She sucks her thumb when she sleeps, but now it's just outside her mouth, like it popped out in her sleep. Her big round head, her little rump sticking up in the air. Little puss. Don't have bad dreams. But if you do, come to me and I'll hold you. I always will. I'll never say you're too old.

The mountains are beautiful now. It's spring, but now there's still snow, almost blue-white. Sam and I have snowball fights, we horse around. I like it that with Sam I can still be a kid. Sometimes I feel grown-up with Jill and all, but sometimes I just want to hack around, to act silly. With David I always felt I had to be serious, sort of, not really myself. He didn't approve of me when I was silly.

Wow, up here I feel so happy I'm going to explode. I'm so full of love for my baby and my man and these absolutely mind-blowing mountains, there isn't room for anything else, there isn't room for pain or sickness, or fear. Life's too incredibly beautiful.

I hope so much that when Jill grows up there'll still be places like this she can come to, beautiful places that aren't spoiled. I'm not so much into politics, but the thing I care about most is saving our land. I think that's so important. Maybe it's from having grown up here, out West. Oh, it's changed already, I know. And Dad is always talking about how much nicer it was when he was young—he's from Montana and he used to go hunting and fishing with his dad when he was little. Even so, there are still places like this you can go to, and the worst thing would be if ever they disappeared or got polluted . . . I could never go live in a big city like Winona. Of course, she has to for her studies, but I think I'd hate it. Three Forks was too small, there wasn't that much to do. I always wanted to get away, but I'd never want a place with all concrete and no trees as I imagine New York must be.

16

It's morning. Sam's out getting some firewood. He got a pretty good fire going. I can see it out of the corner of my eye as I give Jill a bath. I just bathe her in this iron washtub—it's big enough. I put it on the table so it's steady and can't tip. At home I do her in the kitchen sink, or I used to anyway, she's getting kind of big for that now. Sometimes I like to let her take a bath with me. I just put in a little water, maybe a couple of inches, and I get in first and then I lift her in. She loves it! She has a couple of plastic toys—a frog and a giraffe—and we play with them. Sometimes I get out because I have to, to fix dinner or something, and I wish I could let her stay in. Only they say that's dangerous, she might drown.

She loves her bath, even here in the iron washtub with not much room to move around. I can't let her stay in

17

long, it's too chilly, though near the fire it's not so bad. Her body is so great. She's so round and shiny, and she sits there so squat, like a little Buddha. She seems to love the feeling of me running the sponge over her body. Babies are great that way; when you do something that makes their bodies feel good, they just beam at you. They don't mind showing it, but I think grown-ups feel self-conscious. I still do, a little. Sometimes Sam wants to make love out of doors when we're alone in the mountains, or with the sun streaming in the window, and it took me a while to get used to it.

I wash her hair with a little baby shampoo. She hasn't got much hair to speak of, it's light, so what there is doesn't show much. That and her being fat seem to make some people think she's a boy. I guess, also, I never like dressing her in light pink the way you're supposed to to let people know what sex a baby is. I always hated pastel colors, especially light pink. I like red and bright yellow and shocking pink, real bright, glowing colors. Anyway, I don't think Jill looks like a boy. It gets me mad sometimes. The other day this old couple were admiring her in the store and the man said, "What remarkable eyes he has, very wise. He'll be a great mathematician someday." I just said, "She's a girl!" and he said, "Oh . . ." and I thought: So can't she still be a great mathematician anyhow? I mean, she probably wouldn't either way, but it kind of riled me that when I said she was a girl he looked so taken aback, as though saying her eyes looked "wise" couldn't be right. You are wise, aren't you, pooch?

I like to talk to Jill. I know she can't really understand

18

what I'm saying, but she looks at me like she can. Anyway, she likes to hear me babbling away. "You think one day you'll have long silky curls?" I say, trying to get the soap off her—she's so slippery!—"Then you can be Alice in Wonderland and I'll be the White Rabbit and Daddy'll be the Mad Hatter." She reaches for me, she wants to get out. "Cool it there a minute, hon," I say. "You can't get out with all that soap on you or—"

She just wants to get out, the monkey! Look at her, trying to get up, trying to put her arms around me. Oh well, a little soap won't kill her. I reach in back of me for the towel.

Christ! What's happening? Oh my God, I can't stand up, oh Jesus, baby, don't fall, don't let me drop you, oh God, I'm going to. I scream and Sam comes running in. "Get Jill, is she okay?" I yell. "Is she hurt? Get her! Get her!"

"Are *you* all right?" Sam says.

"Get *Jill!*" I scream. I hear her crying. Oh my baby, be okay, please.

Sam goes and picks her up, wraps her in a towel and brings her to me. She's still crying a little, but she quiets down when I hold her and cuddle her. "Little puss, I'm so sorry, are you okay?" Oh, I know she can't talk. Well, she seems okay. I can't see any place she's hurt. Thank God.

"What happened?" Sam says.

"I don't know."

"Did you slip or something? How did you fall?"

I just look at him. We move over to the couch and sit down. "It was my leg . . . it just seemed to—"

19

"Hurt?"

"Like, collapse. I can't describe it exactly. Like it wasn't there when I went to stand on it."

Sam sits there, looking at my leg. There's still that bump that's been there since November. Sometimes it's hot, like it had a fever. "Listen, we're going back to Riverdale right now, right today. No more of this shit. You're going to a decent doctor, one we'll pay for. No more of this crap with that clinic and that old fogey who doesn't know anything."

He's angry. I can tell by the way he storms out with the washtub and tosses the bath water out the back. I just feel—quiet inside, the way you feel after a thing has happened. When I started falling I was just scared, scared for Jill most of all. Maybe if I hadn't been carrying her, I would have felt the pain more. "Dr. Thompson's okay," I say, sort of under my breath.

"Jesus, come *on*, Kate!"

"You never even met him! How do you know?"

"What's he done but waste our time?"

"He did his best, I guess."

I sit there, watching him throw our stuff together. Jill watches him too. I can feel her getting sleepy as she leans against me. "Listen, I went to the clinic to save us money," I say.

"Sure, great bargain . . . It'll wind up costing ten times what it would've if we'd gone to a real doctor to begin with."

"He *was* real! What do you mean—real? He's an M.D."

"He graduated medical school around nineteen hundred . . . What does he know? . . . Weaver's got this

20

lead on a used bike and now we'll have to use every damn penny on another doctor."

I feel so angry, and so depressed because I think he's right. Why did I keep going when I knew he was no good? Because I didn't want to know? I don't know. "I don't *enjoy* being sick," I say. "I'm not doing it on purpose . . . How do you think I feel, practically killing my baby! Quit blaming me!" I'm almost yelling. Thinking all over again what might have happened to Jill scares me.

"All I'm saying," Sam says, "is that if you'd gone to a decent doctor right from the start, you'd be well by now . . . By waiting six months it's going to take ten times longer to cure. It's going to be ten times as expensive . . . And we can't afford it."

"So, go . . . Nobody says you have to spend your money on me . . . No strings, remember? Just get out."

He says nothing. We just stare at each other.

"What does *that* mean?" he says.

"Leave. Go get your stupid bike . . . I'll cope."

He's watching me. "Will you? . . . Sure, probably you will . . . What am I here for, anyhow? Decoration? Comic relief? . . . Shall I leave? Really?"

I just shrug. "Please yourself."

He takes his guitar, goes into the bedroom and slams the door.

Jill is asleep in my arms. I guess our big scene didn't impress her much. These dumb grown-ups, yelling their dumb fool heads off, she probably thinks.

Oh Christ, I feel scared. Don't leave, Sam. Not now . . . It's funny. Before I met Sam, I think I could've coped. I had this job, kind of a dinky job in this beauty

21

shop. They didn't let me set hair or anything, I just swept up and washed people's hair and stuff. It was this really funny place because it seemed to be just old ladies. Everyone was, like, around seventy years old. They'd come tottering in, one lady even was wheeled in in a wheelchair just to have her hair set. They hardly had any hair, some of them! Just light little wisps. I felt so sorry for them. I mean, what were they getting all dolled up for? Just to go home and sit in some room all by themselves. Some of them seemed to live with their sisters or sometimes with a husband. Only all the time the sister would be taken sick or the husband would have a heart attack or one of them would have some dizzy spell. Really, there was almost no day when I didn't hear one of those stories. It was kind of morbid, I guess, only at the time I didn't think of it. I felt so good, being pregnant with Jill. I guess I was like in a screen, in my own world, just daydreaming, not really caring too much.

But now I need Sam, I've gotten used to him, I love him. Would I cope? Yeah, I guess. I'd have to. But I'd hate it. I wish I could say that to him, but I can't. Too much pride, I guess. I say it through the slammed door. Don't leave, honey.

Dr. Jack Lincoln is different from Dr. Thompson. Not as old. Sort of solid and graying, with glasses. Not so nice. Not mean, just kind of stern and factual. He comes out with the X rays and shuffles through them. I have the feeling he's stalling for time.

"Well, there seems to be the possibility of cancer here."

It's the first time anyone has said that word, and it freezes me clear through. It's as though I knew he was going to say it, but hearing it is still so much worse than just imagining it. I just stare at him; I can't think what to say.

"I would suggest you go immediately to the hospital in Spokane for further tests."

I force my lips open, but my voice comes out very low. "Spokane?"

23

"They have the best facilities there . . . You have to have more tests . . . We just aren't equipped here to—"

"But I have a little baby!"

"You'll have to make arrangements for that."

My mouth is so dry, I can't speak. "This other doctor I went to, Dr. Thompson, said it might be bursitis."

"I'm afraid Dr. Thompson was utterly mistaken."

"Why did he say it then?"

Dr. Lincoln shrugs. "I haven't the slightest idea, ignorance, probably."

"But shouldn't—I mean, if a doctor doesn't know, shouldn't he say that? Why should he pretend?"

"Mrs. Williams, let's focus on the present, shall we? Doctors aren't infallible . . . I'll call Dr. Wilde and tell him to expect you in a day or so."

"Okay, sure." I don't want to get up. It's like I know what lies ahead won't be good. This is bad, but it's the beginning. I want to just sit here. I don't want to go to Spokane. I almost wish I hadn't come to Dr. Lincoln, oh that's foolish, I know. But . . .

When I get out of the hospital, carrying Jill, there's Sam in his crazy old VW bus, all painted up with crazy designs on it. He opens the door and leans out. "Need a ride, pretty lady?"

I get in and close the door.

"Where are we going?" Sam says.

"Spokane . . . for tests. He thinks it's a tumor."

Sam looks so scared it scares me all over again. "Look, it's just a tumor, a mole, nothing!" He doesn't say anything. I can't get myself to even say the word "cancer." "I've got to be there Monday."

24

Say something, Sam! Oh Christ, I feel so scared, it just hit me. I'm going to cry, don't let me, I'm crying. "Don't bail out, Sam. Not now."

He reaches over and hugs me tight, holds me. "Do you need the bus fare, girl, or do you need me?"

I started to laugh, even though I'm still crying. "How can anyone be so stupid? How can I love anyone as stupid as you?"

Sam starts to laugh too. And Jill, seeing us both laughing, gives a big, toothless grin. What's the joke, Mommy and Daddy? What's so funny? You're too young to understand, baby. Just too young, that's all.

It's a pretty long drive to Spokane. A day and a half. Jill is real good, sleeps a lot. She seems to like looking out the window. I jiggle her up and down when she gets fussy. But I can't really think about her. I nurse her, but I keep thinking of what lies ahead and that's all I can think about. It's like being in some tiny room and on all the walls are the same thing so no matter how you turn, there it is. There's no door, you can't get out.

Sam said we should've left Jill with his parents. They live just outside Riverdale. I don't know. I guess we could've. But I want Jill with me. She's so important. Without her I don't feel like myself. Also, I know this sounds petty, but Sam's mother bugs me. I know she disapproves of our not being married, that to her, I seem like some loose woman who's living with her precious son. She knows I was married before, that Jill

26

isn't illegitimate, but I know she thinks she is. Unless I brought David around to the house and introduced him to her, she wouldn't really believe he ever existed. She thinks I'm some kind of hippy because I wear my hair loose and wear sandals—oh, all that crazy stuff. Maybe all parents are like that.

I think it's worse because Sam is an only child. She had him late in life. She'd been married fifteen years and trying all the while, I guess, and along he came. So he's like Mama's little baby, even though he's twenty-two. Sam is pretty good about it, I must say. He kind of jokes with her, he sees her faults, he doesn't idealize her. But I think he also doesn't see how much she disapproves of me. He doesn't want to, I guess. When I told her I was having natural childbirth, she kind of stared at me like I'd said I was going to go out in the fields and squat and have the baby on a pile of grass. And the fact that Sam wanted to watch she thought was even crazier. In her day, the Daddy was kept far, far away. He might faint or something. Anyway, I think she also feels a man shouldn't see a woman "like that," meaning real, sweating, in pain. It all ought to be prettied up. Like the baby ought to be cleaned off and powdered. And the Mommy too. Otherwise, "they" lose respect, or some such crud.

Tests and more tests. X rays, electrocardiograms, biopsy. From the time I enter the hospital, it's like my life, my real life—Jill, Sam—is put aside like some old bag. They move me back and forth, cart me around. None of it hurts exactly, it's the fear. I'm being a coward, I know. I shut it all out, as much as I can. David used to say that I had movies going in my head. I do, kind of. When I'm alone or on a bus or at the dentist, I just pull out one of my home movies and start watching it in my mind. It's great. I forget about everything. Sometimes, it's just made-up things, sometimes real things, things I like remembering.

Like the day Sam and I met. I was so happy then. It was this gorgeous perfect day, hot, springtime. I was about four months pregnant, but I didn't show yet. No one knew. I was up in the mountains with some kids, friends. I didn't know most of them real well, just to hack around with. Everyone was spread out on the grass, eating or playing music. I felt—I can't even describe it, but it was a mixture of being where it was so beautiful, the lovely day, being free—I'd left David about six weeks earlier—but mostly, being pregnant with Jill. I felt like Superwoman, like I could do anything; I was bursting with happiness. I liked the fact that no one knew I was pregnant yet but me, that I had this great terrific secret all to myself.

I never had morning sickness the way Darleen seemed to always have. I felt different, sleepy sometimes, but good, strong. I remember exactly where I was standing the minute I saw Sam. I was right outside the cabin handing this basket of bread around, and I just happened to look up and there was Weaver and this guy I'd never seen before pulling up on their bikes, guitars and stuff strapped on the back.

It was basically one of those dumb, crazy moments that you hear about, where you look at someone and you just "know." I mean, I guess love at first sight, except I don't believe in that. I don't believe in it but it happened. Oh, I know sometimes you feel that and you turn out to be dead wrong, the guy is some jerk. Sam isn't even so great-looking. I mean, I love the way he looks, but I've met lots of handsomer guys who I didn't care about at all. I don't really like it if a guy is too handsome, not just because they're stuck up about it, but it's sort of lifeless, these guys with perfect teeth and hair. Sam had this wonderful, slow, kind smile and beautiful eyes, very warm, as though just seeing me had made his day. I smiled right back at him. Mom always used to say I shouldn't smile so much because my teeth are too big. When I smile, you see all of them practically, but I can't help it. I like to smile. I wanted him to know how I felt.

"Well, if it isn't old foul mouth himself," I called out. "Where you been, Weaver? It's been heaven without you."

"Mutual, baby," Weaver said. "You know Sam Hayden?"

"No, but I think I should."

Sam laughed, took his guitar and headed for the cabin. "Let me get a glass of water first," he said.

"I'll get it for you," I said.

"I'll get it."

"No, I'll get it." We ran in, kind of laughing, and I got there first, ahead of him, and gave him this big dipperful of water. I'm not always like that, if I meet a guy I like. Sometimes I'm much more shy and awkward. But it was being pregnant, it was everything. I just felt good, like there was no need to not show how I felt, not to be honest.

I think I kind of made Sam nervous. Now he says it made him feel great, but he looked a little like: wow, who *is* this girl! But he liked me, I could tell.

He sat down and began playing his guitar. It was the first time I heard him play. It was beautiful. I mean, I'd have loved him anyway, but I loved the way he played, the way he held the guitar. I just sat there, staring at him, looking at his face, his hands.

"You come on like this with everybody?" he said.

"Does it embarrass you? . . . It shouldn't."

"Why not?"

I liked that he was embarrassed. I liked teasing him and I knew he liked me. It was so good, that moment before anything had happened, when it was all ahead. Not that what's happened since hasn't been good, but that's the time I love to think back on. "Can I sit there?" I said finally. It was crazy, I just felt I wanted to be near him, to touch him. I guess I was coming on pretty strong, but at the time it didn't seem unnatural at all.

I sat next to him and he kept playing, but I could tell he was nervous. He kept looking at me and shaking his head. Later, Sam said he was feeling how come this had happened to him, what had he done. He said he couldn't quite believe it. Not that he hasn't had girls before, but, well—maybe it was more where he had to make a big play for them, which he says he hates to do. While we were sitting there, some people came in, and they'd look at us and then kind of edge out. I think we looked so happy, it embarrassed people.

Afterward, we took a long walk out in the mountains, just to get off by ourselves.

"What a place!" Sam said. "You been here long?"

"Here at the cabin? Don't I wish . . . I live in Riverdale, but I was born in Three Forks. You know Three Forks? It's right on the Columbia."

"I know," Sam said.

"I left home when I was sixteen," I said. "I was kind of a nervy little brat."

Sam smiled. We were lying on the grass. "I know, I know!" he said, and we were kissing and rolling around in the grass. I knew we'd make love, maybe right then, maybe that night, it didn't seem to matter when, it was

31

gonna happen and be great. But I felt I had to tell him first about the baby. So I pulled away a little. He said later that when I did that his heart sank, because he hadn't figured me for a tease and he was afraid I was going to suddenly come on different—about how we ought to wait till we knew each other better and all that.

"I have to tell you this one thing," I said. "I mean, I want you to know because I think—well, that people should be honest with each other about everything."

He kind of groaned and said, "If we have to be honest, I want you so goddamn much, right this minute!"

"I'm married—I mean I was, and I'm pregnant." I looked right at him. Some guys, that would turn them off. And if he was going to be one of them, I wanted to know right away, not after. Because after, it would hurt too much. I never could just sleep with a guy without falling in love, and I don't think that's bad, only—well, it makes me be more careful.

Sam sat up and looked away. I just sat watching him. It was so important, that moment, telling him. Because I knew I would find out something important about him too, and I just prayed it would be what I'd want.

"Who was it?" he asked.

"Why does everyone ask you *that* first? . . . That's such a dumb question! Ask me if I'm happy!"

"Was it Weaver?"

"Are you *kidding?* He's my cousin, and besides, I hate him. It's nobody here. I haven't seen him since I . . ." I was going to say ran away, but that sounded too young,

32

like a kid, so I added, "since we were separated . . . I married him when I was sixteen. To get away from my mother, I guess."

"What about the baby?"

I lay back on the grass and looked up at the huge, blue sky. "Oh well, that's a whole other trip," I said, smiling.

"You're going to have it? You're going to keep it?"

I looked at him. "Sure I'm going to keep it . . . I want to be a mother more than anything else in the world. I always have."

I didn't mind that he asked me all those questions and that things right away got serious between us. I mean, we could have just gone off and made love and it would've been great and I could've told him then. But I liked that when we finally did make love—he knew, and it was like it was the three of us, making love together, the baby and me and Sam, all together. Being pregnant just made it special. It really was like it was our baby.

It probably seems crazy that I never told David I was pregnant. In fact, even crazier, it was the day I found out I was that I decided to leave him. You'd think it would be the opposite, that when you find out you're pregnant, you get scared and need security and figure— why not give a not-so-good marriage another try. But I didn't feel that way. I felt stronger. Before I was pregnant, I felt weak, like anything David said made me feel so bad or so good. But after I knew, I felt: The hell with you. Maybe I'd felt that deep down all along and it took being pregnant to make it come out. I didn't marry David just to get pregnant. I really was in love with him or thought I was when we got married. But even when things weren't so good with us, I still wanted a baby. And I guess it sounds selfish, but I didn't want to share it with him. I never told him, even when I left that note for him and walked out. It wasn't because I thought he'd holler and yell and try to convince me I had to stay. He would've, but it wasn't that. It was like as long as I didn't tell him, it was just my baby, not his, not a part of our marriage. Sort of the same way I *did* want to tell Sam. I feel really good that Sam was the first person to know. It was something happening to the two of us, even if he hadn't "done it." That didn't seem to matter. Jill is Sam's baby, she really is.

Sam was so good when I gave birth. He was really interested and read all the baby books with me. He even read the part about how to deliver a baby at home just in case it came fast, which luckily Jill didn't. He didn't mind that I got too fat, he said I was beautiful. I knew I was too fat at the very end—I even had to take my rings off because my fingers got swollen—but I didn't mind it. I would have minded, not being pregnant, but I guess at the time I felt like a real earth mother, and I'm not at all that type usually. Usually, I'm skinny and built more like a kid.

They let Sam stay with me while Jill was being born. He sat right near me and joked around and told stories and held my hand. This one bossy nurse kept trying to get him to leave. She said he'd make me nervous, and I said he wouldn't. He kept teasing her. Every time she came in, he'd pretend to hide and say, "Don't make me go, nursie . . . Pretty please. I'll do anything you say." I love it when Sam clowns around. He can be like a child sometimes, but I get a kick out of it, like when he's happy and he'll jump and dance all around.

Now that Jill's six months old, I think back and wonder why I didn't worry more about things like: Would she be born blind or deaf or with six toes? I just didn't. It never occurred to me I wouldn't have a perfect, beautiful baby girl. And I did! When they showed her to me, she was all slimy and wet and my heart kind of sank. I know newborns aren't pretty, but she looked so bad, I just kind of mumbled: Take her away. Thank God they didn't.

Right after I gave birth, it was early morning and Sam went home to sleep. I should've been tired, I'd been up all night, but I was so high, I couldn't sleep. I've smoked grass and stuff, but I never had a high like the one I felt after Jill was born. It was weird, almost. I remember they brought me these magazines, just regular women's magazines which I wouldn't usually even bother to look at. But I would sit there and everything in the magazine would seem fantastic to me. It's hard to describe, but it was like the fact that there was such a thing as a magazine seemed amazing, and the colors, the faces of the people in the ads . . . I'd sit there reading some recipe for chicken and it would leap out at me, I'd want to cry, it seemed so beautiful. It was tiring. I don't even know if I'd want to feel like that all the time. And I didn't. About two weeks later, I started coming down, slowly, not with a hard thump. I never felt depressed the way they say you can. But it was like, suddenly, magazines were just magazines again, the sky was just the sky. I could remember what it had been like, but I didn't feel it anymore.

They say the maternity ward is the only happy place in the hospital, the only place where people are there because they want to be. That was sure true with me. I loved it. I wouldn't have liked to have my baby at home. The nurses were so nice, so friendly. When they brought Jill in the next day and the nurse handed her to me, I was scared I'd drop her. My hands were almost shaking, I was so excited.

"What do I do? How do I do it? Sam, look at her! She's gorgeous."

The nurse tried to settle Jill in just right. "Keep your arm under her head," she said.

Right away Jill made this little snap at my nipple and began to nurse. I felt so proud! "How does she know what to do? It's incredible! She was only just born!"

"It's hard work for her. She'll fall asleep in a minute. Don't worry if she only takes a little." She smiled at us. "I'll let you get to know each other."

Sam sat there, watching me nurse. We were both so happy, it was like you didn't want to talk because there wasn't anything to say. Just it, just being there, was the whole thing. Sam always starts to horse around when he feels that way—being that happy makes him embarrassed, the same way as that time we met. He said, "She looks like Adolf Hitler."

I laughed. "She looks like David."

There was sort of a silence and I wondered if I should've said that, even if it was true. I didn't want David to intrude on the three of us, even by mentioning his name; it just came out.

36

"Speaking of which," Sam said, "they gave me the birth certificate to fill out . . . Where they said 'name of father,' since I didn't know David's last name, I put Sam Hayden . . . Is that all right?"

I wanted to cry. I could feel tears in my eyes and I just reached up to hug him with the hand that wasn't holding Jill.

"All right," I whispered. "Oh wow. That's beautiful."

Someday I'll have Sam's baby. I want to so much. A little boy, a little girl, I don't care which.

I never pretend that Sam and I are married. Someday maybe it'll happen, maybe not. I don't want Sam to ever feel he has to stay with me, out of duty or responsibility or anything. I felt that with David. That because I was so young and he'd taken me from the bosom of my family and all that, he felt I was like his responsibility. I can cope. I know I can. And if there isn't love between us, then let it be over. Maybe I say that now and later I won't, but I think I mean it.

Having been married, I know it isn't everything. It isn't nothing either. I'm not one of those people that feels marriage is dead and the thing to do is just go from one man to the next or be married four times. No, I like the idea of being with one man all my life, till I'm seventy or eighty or something, being a grandma or even a great-grandma. I don't mind the humdrum part of being with someone day after day. David thought it was that. He thought I was too young and I just wanted excitement and wasn't "mature enough." No, you were wrong, David. I like having the same guy come home to me every day and cooking for him and loving him. I mean, sure, I know after a while you feel attracted to other men and you know if you would sleep with them, it would be good, but knowing you can't, that doesn't bother me. So I can't. If what you have is so good, like with Sam and me, it seems greedy to want any more. That's how I feel.

Love came softly
lowered its head,
you are my desire,
come to my bed.

I followed an old road
and once 'round the bend
was met by an army,
come lend me your hand.

I fought many wars,
spent time with a wound,
have cried in the evening,
watched old flowers bloom.

'Tis time I shall leave thee,
watch sunsets from other shores,
and regret not giving
my love even more.

It's lunchtime. The tests are all over. I'm sitting here looking at my lunch and I see Dr. Wilde coming toward the bed. I get this strange feeling. It's like when I was little and we were in the car and I thought the trees were moving. Daddy said—no, it's the car that's moving, the trees are really standing still. But I could see them coming at me, there was no way to stop them coming, I was sure *they* were the ones that were moving. I don't want Dr. Wilde to keep on walking over to my bed, to start talking, and I know he's going to, no matter what. I'm not God, I can't stop him.

He's Chinese, I guess, sort of longish hair, black eyes. Is he married? Does he have a baby? He's coming over, he's looking at my lunch.

"Want some tapioca?"

Without smiling, he says, "It looks delicious."

39

"Yeah." Say it, I'm watching him, I'm ready.

"You kids like it straight from the shoulder, don't you?"

I nod. Am I a kid? No, I feel older than that, but I must look like a kid to him.

He says, "You have something called osteogenic sarcoma. A tumor on the bone."

All those words are so scary, even though I'm not sure what they mean. I say, "But some tumors aren't so bad, right?" My voice is so low, he comes closer to hear me.

"This one's malignant. We need to stop it immediately . . . I've rearranged my schedule and I'll operate tomorrow . . . Osteogenic sarcoma is a kind of cancer that travels from bone to lung. If we do not stop it in the bone, we cannot stop it in the lung."

I lean back against the pillow. "Okay . . . I see."

"Time is of the utmost importance," he says.

"Once it gets to the lung, I die, right?"

"Right."

There aren't any words, just a space, just a vacuum with fear floating around it, crashing around the sides of the room, like a blind person.

"How do you take a tumor out of a bone?"

He hesitates a second. "We take the bone off."

"My leg? You take my *leg* off?"

"It's the best way to try and stop the cancer."

"No! You can't!" The words just leap out of me from somewhere deep inside. Say something else. Please!

Very calmly he takes some papers out of his pocket and puts them on the bedside table. "I'm afraid you have no other options, Mrs. Hayden . . . You'll have to sign these and give them to the nurse."

"What do they say?"

"That you give us permission for the operation."

"But I . . . I have to talk to my—husband. I can't sign anything unless—where is he? Is he out there?"

"I didn't see him."

I hobble out to the hall. Sam isn't there. Oh God, Sam, Christ, where are you? Why aren't you here? What else is more important? I feel frantic. I need you, you bastard! Be here! Why did I say my husband? How petty, how dumb. Why should I care if that doctor knows we're just living together? Maybe *he's* living with someone. Is my lover out there, this guy, this person I happen to love? Sam!

I can't find him, he's gone. Maybe for good. He's split, he's taken Jill. He doesn't want to face it. I don't blame him. Why should he? *I* have to, but he doesn't. He's going to just go, that's it.

God, that doctor, Doctor Wilde, was so cold! Just—cut off your leg! No other option. I mean, there's got to be. In this day and age, with all those medicines they have! He didn't seem to give a damn. Oh, why should he, I guess? Who am I to him? I don't even know if he's right. What if they cut off my leg and it turns out they could've done something else?

Waiting for Sam. He's got to come. He will, won't he? Deep down I don't think he's split. I just said that, thought it. He'll come back. I'm in a ward with some other patients—one has polio, another one had his appendix out, another has a broken hip. God, there are so many ways to be sick, to be deformed, to die. So many ways. I don't want to think about it, I don't want to even be here.

41

I get dressed. I have to keep off my leg, it hurts. I feel weak, kind of. Maybe all the blood they took for the tests. And I've been losing weight. I know I'm thinner; I haven't weighed myself, but I can tell. My pants are loose around the waist. I feel frantic, I've *got* to get out of here! I hate this place!

All of a sudden Sam comes in, carrying Jill.

"Finally!" I say. I hear my voice, too shrill. I'm shaking, I'm so angry, upset.

"What's up?"

"Why weren't you *here?* I needed you!"

He holds me, tries to calm me down, but it doesn't work. I feel like I'm going to explode if I don't get out of here, right this second!

"Hey, hang on, lady! Slow down . . . what's going on?"

"They want to amputate my leg."

He stiffens. "No."

"Tomorrow."

"Come on—"

"Right, big joke . . . Sam, let's get out of here, okay? Please, right this second, right now. I've gotta think, I've got to get up to the mountains."

"What do they want to amputate your leg for?"

"Because it's full of *cancer,*" I yell.

Oh, it's not Sam's fault. Why am I yelling at him? It's no one's fault, but least of all is it Sam's. But I want—someone to share the pain, to help me take it.

That's what Mom always said. Whenever things go wrong: take it easy, but take it . . . take it.

A summer's pasture
at my gate
beckons me astray—
to places found
in lovers' dreams
and easy winter days.

Sky of liquid
dyed-blue scenes
follow close upon my mind,
long dark trains
of empty clouds
and simple musical strains.
Lots of fruit and willow trees
follow from behind.
dreams.
Dreams.

The mountains are so beautiful. It's hot, there are flowers all around. The whole hospital thing didn't happen. This is what's real. How could this be real and that too? It can't be.

We go out with Jill during the day and she crawls around with no clothes on. There's the smell of the flowers, the sound of bees and grasshoppers.

I wonder if there's a God. "Well honey," I remember Mom saying when our old dog, Grey, got hit by a truck. "He had to die sometime and God will be so glad to have such a big nice doggie in heaven."

I was six at the time and I'd seen it happen, seen these people in an old pink Rambler purposely swerve over to hit my dog.

"Does everybody go to heaven, Mommy?"

"Yes, honey, and someday you will too. Just always remember that God will be waiting for you, and there is nothing to be afraid of . . ."

Much as I wanted to believe her, I was scared as hell. I didn't want to go up there and see old Grey, even though I missed him.

How am I supposed to react? What do I do? Should I cry? Just keep going, I guess. If thousands of Jews can burn in ovens and young men can go to war, somewhere in this heart of mine there'll be the courage to go on. There has to be.

I lie here, and the sun is so hot and my baby is so beautiful, and Sam . . . Maybe that time in the hospital was a dream, like that one I had that night. It was last night and now I've woken up.

Sam puts a daisy chain on my head.

"Where did you learn to make those?"

"Girl scout camp."

I laugh and lean back. "The sun feels good."

"Dr. Wilde said a lot of heavy stuff there."

"He's a freak."

"You want to go to another doctor?"

"I don't want to talk about it."

"Every doctor we've seen's said something different . . . Maybe we should go to the Niles Clinic."

"In Vancouver?"

"So, a couple of hundred miles, that's not so much."

"I want to stay right here, just like this, for the rest of my life. I'm happy . . . Oh, shut up, okay?"

He looks away and pulls some sandwiches out of the basket. "Want a peanut butter and jelly?"

"I want some peace and quiet."

He takes out his camera and starts taking photos. Sam takes great photos. I never could. We have some wonderful ones of Jill. We found this great way to get her to laugh for a photo. You just hiccup. She thinks that's a riot. She laughs like a baby hippo, with her whole mouth open.

"Baby, you're getting kind of fat," Sam says.

"What do you mean? She only has three chins."

"I think there's a fourth one sneaking in there."

He keeps snapping away. Jill crawls over on my stomach. "She is kind of heavy, now that you mention it . . ."

"Hold her . . . There, that's it, that's terrific."

She begins picking at my daisy chain. "All your hard work, honey."

He smiles. "I'll make another one."

"Should we let her eat the petals? Is it good for her?"

45

"Sure, it's good. It's great. Nothing like daisy petals to make a baby grow up nice and strong."

Am I not going to see my baby grow up? I never thought of that before this second. No, why would God do that? He doesn't need me, why should he bother? I remember this poem we learned in school by Edgar Allan Poe, "Annabel Lee." She died and he said the gods were jealous of them. Are you jealous of us, God? Don't be. We fight, we have problems, we don't have much money, Sam doesn't even have a job. You don't have to be jealous of us.

Sam is looking at me. "Sweetheart."

"Are we too happy? Is that why?"

"Uh uh." He lies down next to me and holds my hand. The three of us lying in the sun. It's real, we have it now, forget about the rest.

I believe there is a God, but I don't know why I do. Just because it's been harped at me all my life? Maybe. Also because I've seen things happen that I can't explain. I believe that Jesus might have really lived and those things they say he did might've really happened. But I don't know about heaven. I think Jesus meant we had to love each other on earth because earth is our heaven. Earth is imperfect, but it has to be. I don't think we'd want some perfect place, some heaven with streets paved in gold and water sparkling out of streams. It has to be here, if it's anywhere.

I think I'm too human to even enjoy a place like heaven is supposed to be. I wouldn't enjoy "perfection." I like making mistakes, learning from them. I like knowing what's happening. I learned from being married to David, even if it didn't work out.

46

I know we'll have to go back to some hospital, maybe the one in Vancouver. I can't wish it away. But I want these days to sink in, as deep as they can. When we're making love, I want to feel every second, more than I did before. I want to show Sam I love him. Even if he wants to split after this, if things get worse, okay. Let him. I'll understand. I don't want him to feel my love as a burden, dragging him down. I just want him to know someone loved him this much. I want him to have that. Because he deserves it, he's so good, he's so kind.

I wish this weekend could be forever. Just walking around, going barefoot, wearing buttercups in my hair. Getting up at dawn and watching the sun rise: Letting Jill root around in the grass. Everything is new to her now. She'll sit there holding a flower and just staring at it. Babies must be stoned all the time. She just sits and looks and turns it over. No sense of—gee, I'm wasting time, I ought to be doing something else. I learn so much from her. I think babies are wise.

One night we take a blanket outside and lie looking up at the sky, the stars. There're shooting stars now, lots of them. If you lie there like that, the sky is so big, you feel so little.

"Listen, Sam—"

"Umm."

"If . . . well, if you want to split, do it now, okay? I don't mind, I really won't . . . I can get to Vancouver."

"You really think a lot of me, huh?"

"No, I don't mean it that way . . . I just want you to feel free."

"I do."

"No, like, sense of responsibility . . . like you used to

say when your uncle was dying and it took so long and your aunt had to—"

"Honey, this is different."

"It might not be." I wish I could say this right, my words come out all wrong. "Well, just promise, if you ever want to go, you will, right?"

"Sure." He's holding me and the blue-black sky seems like the whole world. If I could die now. No, I don't want to. Even if I could, I still . . .

"I hope I can still have more babies . . . Do you think I can?"

"I just don't know, honey."

"I could get pregnant right away . . . No, Jill's too little, it wouldn't be fair to her, I guess . . . I want to be with her more . . . What do you think the perfect age gap would be? Maybe two years."

"That sounds good."

"I don't care about getting married, that doesn't matter . . . You'd be great with a little boy."

"Yeah, I'd like that."

I can imagine Sam with a son so well. He'd be gentle. He wouldn't make him feel he had to act rough and tough to be a man. He'd teach him just the right way to be. He'd show him things. He'll do that with Jill too, of course, but I think he'd be especially good with a boy. He'd have curly hair, like Sam. He said he was a redhead when he was little. I love real carroty-red hair.

Sunday's our last day. Monday morning we're heading for Vancouver. It's a good day, we're outdoors all the time. Jill's getting a sunburn, but not too red. She doesn't seem to have a delicate skin, even though her hair is light. I put some baby oil on her just to be careful.

As we're coming home for supper, I see someone sitting on the bench in front. It's David. I can tell right away the second I see him, even though he's turned away. How did he get here? How did he—No, dammit, I don't want him here!

Sam, in his usual way, gives a big smile, "Peace . . . Welcome . . . What's your name?"

He could be someone come to kill us, Sam . . . Why does he always expect people to be nice? "It's David," I say under my breath.

"No, can't be," he says, loud enough for David to

49

hear. "He doesn't have fourteen heads and green scaly skin."

That's so much like Sam, to say something like that loud enough for David to hear. Maybe to Sam I have made David out worse than he was, I'm not sure. Just to justify my leaving. I don't think leaving itself was so bad, but maybe it was childish just going off, leaving a note. Only I had tried to explain before that, I'd tried a million times and David just wouldn't listen. He just never took it seriously. If he had, if he'd even bothered to argue with me or discuss it, maybe we'd still be together. In that way I'm almost glad he didn't because then I'd never have met Sam.

David just sits there, watching us come closer. I feel like some big hand in my stomach is tightening up. Go away, David! Vanish into a cloud of smoke.

"What'd you come here for?" I say, trying not to sound angry, trying to be calm.

"To see my child," he says, fixing me with a stare. Why does he do that to me? He makes me shrivel up inside with that look. I hate it.

"She's not yours . . . She's mine," I say, knowing I sound childish.

"Your mother told me about her," he says. "It never occurred to her that I didn't know."

Damn her! Why did she have to tell him? She's never even come to see Jill, that's how much she cares about her. What business is it of hers to tell him? It's so crazy. I always felt Mom thought David was too good for me. Can you imagine? I don't think I'd think any man ever was good enough for Jill, but Mom, she practically tried to convince David not to marry me! Like, he didn't know what he was getting into, he should finish his studies first. Not a word about me. Oh, they got along swell. I bet they had a great time talking about me after I left him. I can just picture it, what a mess I am and was, always was, all the crap both of them have had to put up with because of me. Damn them both!

"I signed the divorce papers," David says.

"You've only had them like a year."

"But I signed them before I knew about the child."

"Her name's Jill," Sam says.

"He doesn't need to know her name," I say, angry at both of them, but more at Sam.

"Look, she has a name, she's not 'the child' . . . Why shouldn't he know it?" To David Sam says, smiling, "She's Jill Patricia Hayden . . . Jill for her paternal grandmother, Patricia for Kate's younger sister, and Hayden for me." He cocks his head to one side. "She looks like you. Kate said she did when she was born."

"I'd like to spend some time with her," David says.

"Come on in, then . . . Have some supper with us."

"I'd like that."

Oh, this is wonderful. Sam, what's wrong with you? Can't you see what I'm feeling? How can you be so nice to everybody?

We go inside. I don't say anything. I just stand there, biting my lips, feeling betrayed and alone. Sam genially hands Jill to David. She's so good with strangers she just sits there, smiling. Scream, yell, baby! Oh, everyone is betraying me! No, she's just a baby. He could be the man in the moon to her.

51

I go into the bedroom and Sam goes after me. "Go away," I say.

"Baby, come on . . . Does it hurt to act civilized?"

"It hurts *me*."

"No, it'll be good."

"It *hurts*, Sam!"

He holds me. He's so good, Sam. He can't know what it's like; he's never been married before and I think that is different from just having lived with someone—and I'm the only person he's ever even lived with. You do commit yourself with marrying someone, and it can get ugly in that special way of feeling trapped. Maybe that could happen somewhat the same with living with someone, but I think it would still be a little different.

Supper. I don't talk. What should I say? I just sit there, looking at the two of them and listening to them. It's interesting, if I wasn't so tight inside, to see Sam and David together. David is better looking—I'm sure most women would think that. Even here, even just spreading mustard on his bread he has that thoughtful, serious, I-know-just-what-I'm-doing air. Sam seems kind of funny, clowning around. There's a kind of sweetness in Sam—that might seem a funny word to use for a man, but I feel he wants so much for David and me to make up, like he was our mother or something. Instead of being jealous the way some guys might—this is my woman. No, he'd never do that. That's not his way.

"It ought to be possible, theoretically at least, for two people to love each other," Sam says, "then stop, but still talk. They're still people, right? Why not be honest—just forget all the rest. It's over. Just deal with what's up front, the practical stuff."

"Sure," I say.

David says nothing, just goes on munching on his sandwich.

Sam raises his hand and gestures like an actor. "Never let it be said that man, in the quest of peace and love and understanding, be it ever so humble, quests in vain."

David looks at me with a wry expression. "What's he on?"

"Nothing." I can't help smiling. "He just gets this way."

"Spooky," David says.

"I like it," I say, looking right at him.

Silence again. This is really a great dinner.

"Your car was packed," Sam says. "Where you headed?"

"Pullman, the university."

Sam looks at David admiringly. "Can you cut that? What're you studying?"

"Geology," David says.

Sam, you're worth ten thousand million Davids no matter how many dumb degrees he has. Don't you know that, you idiot?

David is looking at me. "I talked to a lawyer," he said. "Not telling me you were pregnant when you filed for a divorce is what they call an omission of a material fact . . . which means I don't have to agree to the divorce. And I can get custody of the child."

I just plain don't believe this. No one would be that cruel. I can't even believe he's right. What kind of law is that? To give a baby to her father who never gave a shit about children, who didn't even *want* them. David

53

always said the world was too rotten, he didn't want to tie us down. I always thought maybe if I got pregnant, he'd go along with it, accept it, but he never wanted it, never. "You can't have her," I say.

"Why do you want her, anyway?" Sam says. "Are you big on babies?" He says it in his innocent way, kind of wondering, the way he asked about David's studying. It's a little of an act, Sam's not really innocent. He's putting David on a little.

"I'm not saying I want her," David says. "I'm saying I can have her."

Sam looks at me. "I see what you mean about him."

David won't pay any attention to Sam, like he wasn't there. Maybe he knows I'm more vulnerable. If Sam wasn't here—no. I don't even want to think of that, I'd be screaming, I'd be hysterical. I'm like that inside now, but just having Sam here makes me able to keep it down. "Frankly, I don't know why *you* want a baby," David says to me. "How come you didn't have an abortion?" To Sam he says, "All I heard for a year and a half was—lemme out! I'm trapped, this is an awful mistake, I'm tied down, I hate making your bed, ironing your shirts, I hate responsibility, I'm not ready—"

"Shut up!"

I hate David when he gets going like that. He can massacre me with words, relentless, going at me, distorting everything. "Here you are, taking care of a house, a man, and a child . . . What happened? What was the great miracle?"

"I wear T-shirts," Sam says.

"I grew up," I say. I could say: It's different when you love someone, but aside from being cruel that isn't even true. I mean, it's not the real difference. It's that Sam doesn't care about those things, he doesn't make me feel like I'm a person he bought to do chores around the house and he'll fire me if I don't act right. Partly, he just doesn't care about all that, the way David did, does, but also he feels it's my thing. If I want to—fine. And once you don't feel you have to, it's not a burden. I really like housework, crazily enough. I mean, not to spend all day at it, but I like the house to be clean and nice, so long as I don't feel someone is making me or will be angry if one morning I want to lie in bed and write a poem instead of defrosting the refrigerator.

"I'm really impressed," David is saying. "No, it's a real miracle . . . To grow up in one year from a little, whiny kid to—"

"Why did you marry me if I was a little, whiny kid?"

"You weren't like that when I married you!"

"Well, maybe—"

"Hey, kids, cool it," Sam says.

We both glare at him.

"I mean, I don't like to be insulting," Sam says, "but speaking of little kids, you two are not exactly—"

"Look, maybe Kate is a great mother right now," David says. "It's possible . . . But what happens when the next great transformation occurs? When some other life-style strikes her fancy? Then what?"

"That's unfair," Sam says.

"Is it fair to raise a child when you're stoned on grass or whatever half the—"

I get up. "I don't believe this . . . That's the stupidest thing I've ever heard! It's not even true!" As though I was some hippy out of a book. He sounds like

55

my mother. Either you're straight and narrow or you're a wild, drooling, grass-smoking maniac who's a danger to little babies. How did I marry someone like this?

"I'll give you the divorce, if you'll give me Jill," David says. "I'll raise her right. My mother will. You know her, Kate. You like her. She'll raise her right, won't she? . . . And you'll have what you've always wanted. Freedom. A new start. No responsibilities."

I start to cry. He can't do that, he just can't. He can't take my baby. I won't let him.

Sam says, "Listen, Jill needs Kate, Kate needs Jill. I need them both . . . Does that make sense to you?"

"Why don't we go outside and talk it over?" David says.

"You're kidding, come on . . . why can't we talk here? This involves Kate."

"I'd rather do it my way," David says.

Sam makes a comic face and straggles out after David.

They're going to kill each other. Oh, how dumb, how awful. Please God, I know I said I don't believe in everything about you like heaven and all that, but if you exist, don't let him take Jill. Okay? I won't ask for any other thing, I promise. Just that.

I walk in and look at her. She's sleeping on her back. Babies sleep in such a vulnerable way, on their backs like that with their arms and legs spread out, like a puppy wanting you to rub his stomach. She's in a little pink stretch suit, which is getting tight around her neck because of her chins. I guess she needs an extra large already. She never has a blanket—she just kicks it off, and the stretch suit is wool, it's warm enough. My puss, he never even said anything about you, he never said how pretty, how good. He just held you like a sack of potatoes.

Sure, I like David's mother. I do, really. I like her more than David actually. Maybe because I think she thinks he's kind of a square too, kind of rigid. And he thinks she's kind of kooky because she goes on marches against the war and says she was a feminist before her time. She is great, but she's—well, she's sixty and that's too old! And even if she were forty, that's not the point. I want my baby. Maybe he's right. Maybe when I was with him I was all those things, but I am different now. Why can't he see that? Because he doesn't want to think it was him who was making me that way?

He doesn't want Jill! He doesn't even want her! He wants to hurt me, that's all. I don't want to hurt you, David. I just want you to go away and never come back. I'm not even asking you for alimony or child support. You're the one who can be free and go live in some nice apartment and travel like you said you wanted and maybe later marry some lady geologist who would give parties the way you wanted. What would *you* do with a baby?

I can hear David's car starting up outside. Well, at least one of them is alive. No, that was silly. Sam doesn't even like fighting. He's said that when he was little, they all made fun of him because he never liked to fight. He wasn't scared, he just didn't believe in it.

He comes back in the house.

"Who killed who?"

"We killed each other."

I start giggling. I feel so happy to have it over, to have David gone. "Come on, tell me, what happened?"

"He understood."

"Really?" Suddenly I look at him. He has a funny expression on his face. "Did you tell him about my—did you tell him I was sick?"

Sam nods.

"Oh Sam, why? Why does he have to know that?"

"I don't know . . . I think it's important."

"You mean, any other time it would be okay for him to take Jill, but not now that I'm sick?"

"No, honey, come on . . . We wanted her, we have her . . . That's the important thing, right?"

"Yeah, I guess." I sigh. "He's sweet, isn't he?"

"Adorable . . . You have wonderful taste in men."

"Wow." I pick up a piece of bread and butter. Suddenly, I feel hungry, I didn't eat anything at dinner.

"Is that what he was usually like?"

I take a sip of wine. "Not every second . . . But I'm glad you saw it. I mean, otherwise you might've thought that I was making it up—"

"No, I wouldn't have."

Good-bye, David. Good try.

The Niles Clinic is the best. We decide to go there and see. It's a long drive again to Vancouver. Sam drives; I sit next to him, holding Jill. She looks out the window, smiles, makes these strange crooning sounds to herself, like a bird. I wonder what she sees. She doesn't know where we're going, that we're in a car, that those are trees, what a mountain is. But it must mean something to her, she keeps talking to herself in her bird language, gesturing her fat, little hands like she was conducting a symphony.

We sing some of the time, we talk. But we don't talk about where we're going or why we're going there. Deep down I know it's not going to be different, it'll be the same tests, the same kind of doctors' faces, cold, straight, not caring. But I feel they have to have some answer besides cutting off my leg. Here there's always all this stuff in the paper about cancer and trying to cure it. They must have gotten further than just saying cut off your leg. If it was my breast—well, I wouldn't mind so much. Oh, I would mind, but—it's not being able to get around, being a cripple. Nobody would see with a breast, except Sam, and he—well, I don't know how he'd feel. But with a leg, everyone could see. Jill would see me that way. Don't let me be a coward. I don't want to be. I just want to grow up and take care of Jill and Sam. That's all. Is it such a huge amount to ask for?

The Niles Clinic is very big. For several days I go through all the tests again. They give me something called a bone scan. They inject a radioactive drug in the vein of my arm. Then a day or so later, they put me under a machine that detects the hot spots or the places where the radioactive material has gone to, which indicates the more active parts of the tumor. I lie there for an hour, I can't tell how long, as still as I can, and this arm of the machine moves back and forth above me, detecting the hot spots and recording them on film.

They take a scintiscan of my liver. It's like having an ordinary black and white Polaroid Color Pack II mounted on a $50,000 computer that can take pictures of anything—the heart, the brain. There, they show it to me—a little black and white snapshot of my liver. Incredible!

I try to run my home movies in my mind, but they keep flickering out and the faces of the doctors come in. I have to tell my story so many times; when I first noticed the bump, what the other doctors said, when the first X rays were taken. Over and over.

They put a crib and a folding bed into my room so

that Sam and Jill can stay with me which is good except that sometimes having Sam around gets on my nerves. I don't feel like joking or even talking. Then, when I do, when I want him, he's not around. Am I going through this every time with him? Here one minute, gone the next? Sam, come on!

Dr. Gillman, the head doctor, sees me in the corridor. "You shouldn't be up, Kate," she says. "You need to keep your weight off that leg."

It's funny to me, a woman in charge of a whole cancer section. I mean, I know women are doctors, but I never went to one or even heard of anybody going to one. Can she be good? How awful, that's so prejudiced, but I wonder if a woman can be as good a doctor, know as much . . . But I like her. She reminds me of my grandmother, Dad's mother, who stayed with us for about a year before she died. That sounds funny, since Dr. Gillman is only in her thirties or something and my grandmother was in her seventies. It's something about her eyes, her voice, very quiet and sure. I used to come into my grandmother's room after school. She'd be sitting there, working on her patchwork quilts. She'd let me help her, I'd trim the patches out and she'd hem them. I think it got on Mom's nerves, having her live with us. She said we didn't have room enough and Grandma was always in her way. But Dad loved her and didn't want to put her in some home where they were all so sick, some with strokes and things like that. It seemed cruel. Toward the end, she got sort of senile. She used to go around wearing maybe six petticoats at once because she was afraid someone might steal her things, and she was always losing things and wandering

61

off and getting lost. I guess she was a bother for Mom, but I always loved her.

"Are you a good doctor?" I say suddenly.

Dr. Gillman smiles. "Very good . . . Why?"

"I never had a woman doctor."

"Don't you think women can be good doctors?"

"I guess I . . . I don't know . . . Did they put you in charge of this part because we're all hopeless cases?"

"Because this is the children's wing." She smiles at me. "Children who don't stay in bed when they're told to stay in bed."

"My bottom gets sore," I say defensively.

"I'll have them bring you a crutch."

"Great."

What I like about Dr. Gillman, compared to that doctor in Spokane, is she treats me like a person. He treated me like a thing, like a "case." I mean, I know all patients are cases to doctors, they can't get personally involved every time, but it makes such a difference when they look at you like they care, like you're important to them, even a little bit.

She comes back after lunch and sits near my bed. "We better talk about your treatment," she says.

I'm so scared again. For a while it went away, now it comes back suddenly, like someone just threw a hood over my head. "Don't cut off my leg," I say. My mouth is dry. I lick my lips, watching her.

"The scanner showed it may not have spread to any other parts of your body which is amazing considering how long you waited."

"I didn't wait, though! I went, only they said—"

"No, I know . . . You did wait a little, however."

62

"I was pregnant, though, and—"

"I understand, Kate . . . And those doctors who told you you had bursitis, that's very unfortunate. That kind of misdiagnosis is still possible. I regret it very much . . . But that's all over. And for now, amputation is your best option."

"Will it get rid of the cancer?"

She hesitates. "It might."

"But if it hasn't spread—"

"It's a chance, Kate . . . I won't lie to you. That's all it is, a chance."

"Why can't they cure it some other way, for good?"

"Someday they will."

"But it won't do *me* any good, right?"

"These things take a long time, finding out what cancer is will take a long time, how to cure it is something else again."

"So I'll be one-legged and dying. Terrific."

"Your only other option is chemotherapy and radiation. Radiation to kill the cancer in the bone. Drugs to stop it spreading to other parts of your body . . . The possible side effects of radiation you know about. From the drugs you may have loss of hair, diarrhea, nausea."

"Will I be able to have more children?"

"No, you won't, Kate. I'm sorry."

"Never?"

"No."

I look away. Don't let me cry, please! Oh Christ, let me be strong, I've got to be! I feel Dr. Gillman's kind, worried eyes on me. I can't speak.

"Kate?"

"Have you noticed that Sam is never here when I

63

need him?" I say suddenly, the words bursting out. "That's true. Never. Mr. Vanishing Act . . . You know where he is? Auditioning. He goes off to some damn audition right when I need him. What's more important, country western music or my life? Country western music, hands down."

"He needs a job, Kate," Dr. Gillman says kindly. "He wants to take care of you. He can't do that without a job."

"But I need him *here!*"

I go out to the phone and try to call the place where Sam's auditioning. I hate phone booths, operators, switchboards. It's so humiliating to keep calling and get no answer. "No, I'm sorry, we don't know where he can be reached . . ." Fuck them! I can't have more children, Sam! I'll never have your baby! Don't you care? Why aren't you here? I lean back and close my eyes.

Suddenly, I see Sam, walking past the phone booth with Jill in the backpack. He doesn't see me. I just sit there and a minute later he comes back. I look up at him.

"You look like you could use some music, lady," he says.

I just glare at him.

"Come back to bed . . . You're not supposed to be up."

"How do you know?" I follow him. I feel so full of bitter, ugly, sad feelings. My leg is hurting. It does feel better to get in bed.

Sam takes out his guitar and begins picking at it. He's put Jill in her crib in a corner of the room.

"I can't make any sensible decision without you and you're never here," I say.

"This morning you said I was getting on your nerves."

"Well, I didn't need you while I was having the tests . . . Any idiot could figure *that* out!"

He keeps strumming on the guitar.

"Stop hiding behind that stupid guitar!"

He's hurt. His face goes blank and he puts the guitar down. "Look, Kate, how much more money do you think I want to borrow from my parents?" he says, angry. "I've got to get a job, I've—"

"Oh, cut it out. You could get a job any day in the week if you wanted. Washing dishes. Mopping floors. Driving a truck. But you don't. You just want to get away. From me, from this whole scene . . . 'Cause you're too weak to—"

"Get away? Right, great, I've just been staying here, sleeping at the foot of your bed ever since you checked in, for fun! I sort of dig hospitals, right?"

"You don't have anyplace else to sleep, for free."

"Quit it!"

Why am I doing this? Oh, I don't need the pain of wrecking what there is between Sam and me. Am I angry just because he isn't sick, because he has so many options, getting a job, not getting one, because he has two strong legs and no one wants to cut either of them off, no one is piping him full of radioactivity.

Jill is fussing and I go to get her. I can feel Sam watching me. I hurt him, I know it. He's angry. Oh, I wish we could just lie down together and love each other like we used to. I can imagine us together, as I'm

65

picking up Jill, it's as though I was with Sam and we were out in some meadow and the sun was shining.

Holding Jill makes me feel good, better anyway. She's so fat and soft and she doesn't hate me or look at me with angry eyes. I snuggle her up to my breast, cradling her. I can't look at Sam, I just can't.

Suddenly, Dr. Gillman comes in. "Don't let her nurse," she says to Sam.

Talk to *me!* It's *my* baby! "But she—"

"You have radioactive iodine in you from the tests. It can be passed in your milk . . . Take her off your breasts."

I pull Jill away and she begins to cry. I feel like I'm dying. Please don't take my baby away! How horrible, that my body is filled with poison, that my milk is contaminated. "I wasn't going to wean her till she was . . . I—"

"I'll get a bottle," Dr. Gillman says.

Jill and I are both crying. She's hungry and frustrated; I feel like I want to curl up and pull the blankets over my head. Oh, it's not fair! Sam stands near the bed, stroking Jill's head. "Should I take her?" he says softly. "Should I hold her?"

"Go away."

"I thought I was never around when you needed me?"

"Get out."

Dr. Gillman comes in with a bottle. She props me up with some pillows. "Sit up more, Kate . . . Now it's perfectly easy. You just hold her as you would if you were nursing, and give her the bottle . . . And stop crying."

I can't stop, the tears keep rolling down my cheeks. Jill doesn't want the bottle. She turns away. Even she's angry at me!

"She won't take it."

"Let me," Sam says.

"No!"

I hold Jill against me. Sam looks at me, incredulous. I see Dr. Gillman glance at him. "You know, it might be a good idea to let Sam feed her, Kate . . . With you she's used to the breast. Babies often take bottles from their fathers and—"

"He's *not* her father," I say bitterly. "He's not my husband, either."

Dr. Gillman takes Jill and gives her to Sam. He sits down with the bottle. "Is this the way?" he says.

"Hold her head up a little more," she says. "There, now look . . . She's used to it already!"

"But it's not the same as nursing," I say.

"Not exactly . . . But the baby feels you love her just as much. Babies aren't dumb. They can tell if they're loved."

I feel jealous, watching Sam feed Jill. She does look perfectly at home in his arms, like he was her mother.

"I thought I understood that Jill's last name was the same as yours?" Dr. Gillman says to Sam.

"It is . . . Kate was married before, but she left her husband before Jill was born."

"She obviously feels you're her father," Dr. Gillman says, smiling warmly.

He smiles back at her. "Yeah, well, I—"

"I actually think bottle feeding has a lot of advantages," she says. "Why should the mother have all the

67

fun? I think it's nice for the baby to get to know that lots of people care about her and love her."

"So, if anything happens to the mother, she won't—" I start to say, but Dr. Gillman says, "Just so she feels all her happiness isn't just one person."

I guess I *want* her to feel all her happiness is me, that's selfish, I know. And Sam does look so sweet, feeding her, so awkward, but sort of pleased with himself. He glances at me just one second, as though to get my approval, and then away. But I still feel too tight inside, I can't let go.

"Have you two discussed your treatment yet?" Dr. Gillman says.

Sam looks at me. "*I'd* like to," he says.

"Well, the generally accepted way to treat osteogenic sarcoma is by amputation. You remove the cancerous part. If it hasn't spread, it's the best solution."

"He's not interested."

Sam makes a disgusted face and looks away.

"The other possibility," Dr. Gillman says, "is radiation and chemotherapy."

"Which will cause my hair to fall out, my leg to break, diarrhea, and nausea," I say, bitter.

"Possibly," says Dr. Gillman, "but I don't know that you can compare losing your hair with losing your leg."

"It's a lousy trip either way," I say, looking at both of them. "Why don't we skip the whole bit?"

They are both staring at me like I'm crazy. I feel crazy, no, not crazy, just full of ugliness, of hate at the unfairness of it. And their kindness makes it worse, somehow. I guess I want to blame someone and they're the only ones patient enough to sit here and listen to me ranting.

"That's suicide," Sam says, his eyes cold and angry again.

Why can't he understand? Is it so clear-cut? Would he just have his leg cut off in one second like that without caring? "But all these horrible things she's going to do to me," I say, my voice shaking a little, "and no guarantees!"

"No guarantees," Dr. Gillman says, "but a little more time." She looks over at Jill who is sucking away on the bottle—she really seems to like it. "Time for this one . . . I thought that's what you wanted—to be a mother."

I curl up in bed, away from both of them, all of them, even Jill. I wish I could explain how I feel. I know they both think I'm acting childish, unrealistic, immature. Okay, maybe I'm too young, so why am I sick, why am I dying? I'm too young for that, so why did it happen? If they can't understand, no one will, and I can't bear that somehow. I can't bear that cold look in Sam's eyes. If only someone could say why this was happening. There is no why, I guess. Do I want there to be? Would that make it better? To have someone say: This is because you were born on the thirteenth, this is because you ran away from home, because you made your first husband miserable, because your mother thinks you're a whore . . . That's childish, to want life to be a matter of "punishment" for one's sins, but to have it just happen, at random, and for no reason, that's almost worse. Oh, I don't know what I want anymore. Except to be left alone, to try and figure it out. I turn around and look at them. "It's just," I try to keep my voice steady, "I don't want to be a temporary mother, for a year or two. I want to be a mother until I'm a grandmother . . . I can't learn to walk on one leg while Jill's learning to walk on two, I won't . . . It's not fair to Jill."

After my big announcement, Jill gives a decisive burp. So much for you and your dramatic words, Mom. Sam pats her back. She looks very pleased with herself.

"What does all that mean, in practical terms?" Dr. Gillman says.

Sam smiles, but he doesn't look angry anymore, his voice is gentle. "It means she wants to wake up tomorrow with no cancer."

I try to joke, too. "And three legs, please. Certainly not any less than two."

Dr. Gillman nods, as though she were satisfied. "Fine. Then we'll start radiation treatment in the morning."

I feel so relieved she understands that I want to cry. I look at Sam. Jill is almost asleep, nodding in his arms. "Can I hold her?"

"Sure." He gives her to me and she settles against me, warm, milky. "She drank the whole thing," he says proudly.

"She's going to be a fat girl, aren't you?" I say, pressing one finger lightly on her cheek. "All that milk . . ."

"Would you two call a truce if I sent in two dinners?" Dr. Gillman says, from the door.

"Sure," Sam says.

"No," I say.

They both look at me, surprised.

70

I smile teasingly. "I'm not hungry," I say.

Dr. Gillman shakes her head. "You're impossible," she says, but in a nice way. I really like her. Maybe all doctors should be women.

After she leaves, Sam comes over and sits right next to me on the bed. I suddenly feel physically aware of him, wanting him. I imagine us together in this bed. He doesn't touch me, just sits very close, but it's as though we were touching. "Why is it tangled up, all of a sudden?" he says.

"I don't know."

He takes my hand and kisses it. There are marks there, from the shots. "I love you . . . Did you forget that?"

"No. It's just that . . . I don't know."

"Say it."

"I'm scared."

"I know . . . I am too. Everybody is, baby, inside, always."

"Maybe she's wrong . . . Maybe there's another doctor somewhere else who'll have another answer."

He frowns, hesitates. "I don't have the money to go anyplace else," he says. "And you don't have the time . . . This is the biggest and the best cancer center in the whole Northwest. Dr. Gillman's the head of it. At least, this part of it. She's got to know something. We've got to trust her, baby. And each other. Ninety-nine percent of this scene is trust."

I know Sam's right. And I do trust Dr. Gillman. There is no other answer, there is no other doctor, the world over probably, with anything else to say.

Sam takes Jill who is fast asleep and puts her in her

71

crib. What a crazy family life, the three of us here. He reaches over and kisses me, holds me. I can feel his heart beating. He looks at me. *"Now* tell me to leave."

"Leave," I say teasingly, smiling.

"And mean it."

I bury my face up against him. "I couldn't . . . Not in a million years."

He kisses me again, then leans back. "Whew . . . We'd better be careful, I guess."

"Dr. Gillman'll be back any second," I say.

"I'm going to find us a place," he says. "You'll be out of here soon, then—"

I just look at him, wanting him, but not so it tears me up. We'll have time together. Sam is right.

He's over by the window, looking out. "Oh, by the way, the divorce papers were in the mail this morning." Very casual.

I let out a yelp. "Wow! Where's the champagne?" I start to laugh, I feel so great. Freedom!

"I'm saving it for the wedding," Sam says.

There's a long pause.

"Sure, in the great hereafter?"

"Tomorrow," he says, straight. "After your first treatment."

Is he joking? He wouldn't, would he? Sam is so funny, I can't figure him out. "My mother used to get us milk shakes after the dentist," I say.

"This is for *real*," he says.

I swallow. "We're going to get married? In the hospital?"

Suddenly Sam looks all excited. "Weaver and I met this guy playing at the audition. He studied to be a

72

rabbi once . . . Want to be married by an almost-rabbi?"

I give a hoot. "My mother will flip out!"

"He's a hundred feet tall and he looks like Moses," Sam says, pleased with himself. "Except his beard's shorter. He'll keep me humble."

I can't quite believe it somehow, it doesn't seem possible. "Sam, you're serious? . . . Is it legal?"

He just grins. "Probably not . . . I'll have a justice of the peace waiting in the wings."

I just look at him, puzzled. I don't want to spoil it, but, "Why now?" I say. "I mean, marrying me's like betting on a three-legged horse. You can't win."

He smiles at me. "Sure you can . . . If you have a thing for three-legged horses."

I have to cry, I can't help it. I'm too happy.

73

David and I were married in City Hall. I was wearing a new dress. It was white, but not fancy. I still have it, I like it. I guess there was a feeling of nervousness about it, knowing my parents didn't approve, and a feeling of anger on my part toward them, like they couldn't stop me, no matter what they thought about it. Pat wanted to come. She was the only one who thought it was great. At night she'd come in my room and I'd tell her all the things about where we would live and what a great housekeeper I would be. I liked telling her because she'd look at me with her big, big eyes. She thought I was wonderful and the whole thing was so exciting and David so handsome.

Actually, I got to know David because of Pat. He was supervising at the ice skating rink and she noticed him and dragged me down to see him. I'm a really good ice skater, I've done it since I was five. I thought he was kind of cute and I got out on the ice and started showing off a little, twirling around in my little red skirt. Well, I was sixteen, what can you expect. He was watching me, I could tell, even though he was supposedly keeping an eye on the little kids, seeing they didn't get into trouble. Only then I fell! I guess I was being a little too much of a show-off for my own good because I twisted around and fell, kerplunk, right on my bottom. I couldn't look at him, I knew he'd be smiling. I just got up and tried to skate gracefully off the ice. And when I was sitting there, feeling my foot to see if it was okay, he came over and sat down next to me and we started to talk.

If I hadn't met David, I wouldn't have left home, and if I hadn't left home, I wouldn't have met Sam. So maybe all those things are tied together in some crazy way. To say nothing of the fact that if I hadn't married David, I wouldn't've had Jill. So I've been kind of lucky when you think about it. I haven't been mistreated or anything.

If I had to be sick, I'm glad I'm here and I'm glad Dr. Gillman is my doctor. I'm so glad we didn't stay in that hospital in Spokane.

Maybe once I get out of here I'll start trying to write poetry again. I'd like to, if I can. I'm not good. Only once or twice I did a few things I liked, but I still like to do it, try to put in a poem how I feel. I really respect people like Bob Dylan and Leonard Cohen who write such beautiful lyrics. In high school I used to write down poems or songs I really liked. Maybe I'll do that again. Get me a nice, fresh notebook. It would be nice

75

to have really pretty handwriting—mine is kind of sloppy. There was this teacher in our school who knew how to write in a special way with special pens and brushes. I would've liked to learn how from her.

I'm getting married again! Sam is going to be my husband. How weird. It's hard to believe.

As the early dawn comes
and i watch your warm body
rise and fall
in soft slumber
i know
your dreams of today must fade,
for today
it will be no better
than before.

Life has brought us to a place
on an old dirt road
in the mountains
and left us with no gasoline for our car.

We must do the best we can
with what has been given us
and live the best we can,
for life is real
and can hurt us if we don't.

Givits, the rabbi Sam met at the audition, is really something. Real tall like Sam said, he comes into the hospital room in a crash helmet, a ratty black shirt, jeans, a fringed vest, gold-rimmed glasses, and a wild beard. Wow, my mother would love him. All her fears about her hippy daughter would be proven in one shot if she ever saw him. Only she won't.

Sam looks beautiful. Can you say that of a man? He does. He has this great shirt he must have bought somewhere, a Mexican shirt. He's washed his hair—it's kind of sticking up the way it does just after he's washed it. I know Sam so well, maybe that's why it seems funny that we're getting married. I never knew David at all, even after we'd been married, as well as I know Sam right this minute.

I washed my hair too. I think I still look pretty. I'm thinner, but it makes my eyes look big. Sam brought some flowers for me to wear in my hair.

It's all so crazy! Jill's asleep in her crib and Dr. Gillman and all the doctors and nurses are crowded into the room. I bet none of them ever saw this before, a wedding in a hospital. Weaver, in his usual stuff, is strumming on his guitar.

Givits takes my hand and Sam's and says, in this very soft voice—"Put the ring on her right index finger."

Sam is really nervous! I can tell because his hands are ice cold. He fumbles around for the ring and puts it on my finger. I feel nervous too. I can't look at him. Givits takes the ring off and gives it back to Sam. "Hey, wrong finger!" he says. To me he says, smiling, "Beautiful women always fall for dumb men, why is that?"

Sam puts it on the right finger, I hadn't even noticed!

"Now, you, Kate . . . You put it on Sam."

I do.

Givits grins. "Great, you're getting the hang of it . . . Now, pay attention to this part, folks. We're getting to the crux, the heart, the soul, the foundation." He looks up at Weaver. "Hey, quiet, okay?" Weaver stops strumming. Givits says, "Repeat after me: Behold, thou art consecrated unto me by this ring."

Sam looks right at me. "Behold, thou art consecrated unto me by this ring."

Givits raises his hand. "Note—consecrated means she becomes holy, an object of reverence and utmost regard. Heavy stuff . . . Okay, time to drink."

We pass the wineglass around and each takes a sip. Weaver begins playing again, but softly.

Givits, in a kind of singing chant, says, "Blessed art Thou, O Lord God, who created joy and gladness, bridegroom and bride, mirth and exultation, pleasure and delight, love, brotherhood, peace and fellowship." He takes the glass and drains it, then puts it on the floor in front of Sam. "Step on it," he says, "smash it."

Sam smashes it. Jill, hearing the sound, stirs in her crib. She sits up, looking at this whole crowd. I can see it from her eyes—who are all these people? Why are my Mommy and Daddy in these funny clothes? Her face is all puckered up, trying to understand.

"Note," Givits says. "As impossible as it would be to put this glass back together, so it is impossible for you to live apart from one another."

Jill begins to cry.

Sam reaches over and hands her to me. I'm glad she's a part of our wedding. I hold her and she quiets down, hanging on to me, looking with big eyes at Givits. He rumples her hair, what little she has. "You almost missed the whole show, sleepyhead," he says.

Then he begins singing again, "Banish, O Lord, both grief and wrath, and then the dumb shall exult in song. With the sanction of those present, we will bless our God, in whose abode is joy, and of whose bounty we have partaken . . . Repeat after me—Blessed be our God—"

"Blessed be our God."

"In whose abode is joy," Givits says.

"In whose abode is joy," we all say except Jill who just stares at this funny man with her big eyes.

"Of whose bounty we have partaken."

"Of whose bounty we have partaken."

"Through whose goodness we live."

Sam takes my hand and we look at each other. I know I'm going to cry in one second, but luckily just then he kisses me and my tears brush off on his shirt. Then there's a lot of laughing and noise and Jill, with an indignant yelp, seeing us all sipping champagne, decides it's time for her bottle.

While I'm in the hospital, Sam gets us an apartment. I'll be going in for treatments off and on so he tries to find one not too far away. Finally, one day, Monday, we all drive up to it—it's a small house with three stories. Jill is trying to walk—she's not a year yet, but you can see she's really determined. Mom said I was an early walker and she never knew what to do with me, I got into everything. Well, let her get into whatever she wants. I don't mind.

"Welcome home, Mama," Sam says.

I limp after him on my crutch. I'm getting used to it, I can manage pretty well with it now. "Which one is it?"

"The bay window that hasn't been washed in thirty-five years."

"Oh Sam!" I can't help being excited. Just to be out

of the hospital, to have our own place again, not to be surrounded every second by doctors and nurses and sick people.

Sam goes ahead, pointing things out. "Indoor plumbing, not too many steps. Close enough to the hospital to walk when you're feeling stronger, and the whole beautiful world out your window."

I kiss him, laughing. I feel so good, so free. I walk around slowly. Sam has set the mattress of our bed on the floor and even tried to make the bed a little, sort of dragged a quilt over it. There's a rocker, some chairs. On the wall some posters. All the stuff from our first apartment. Sam drove down and brought it all up here. It makes me feel good to see our old stuff, though it's not so very beautiful, but I have such good associations with it, with the rocker, with that bed, all the love that started in it. I don't think, even if we got rich one day, I'd ever want to get a new bed.

"It's enormous," I say. "How can we ever afford it? We—"

"Let me worry about that," Sam says. He looks so pleased at having found it, at having set it all up, that I decide not to worry about the money thing just yet.

Even the kitchen isn't bad, though it's small. Lots of cabinets. I think I'll make some curtains, something cheerful in a print. I can pick up some material at the dime store. "I'm going to make a rug," I say. "My grandmother taught me years ago. A rag rug. They're really easy. Then a giant patchwork quilt—"

Jill is running around from room to room with her funny, wide-legged walk. She falls every few steps, but she's so pleased with herself. Sam grabs her and they roll

82

around, she giggling her head off. I love watching them together.

The door opens. It's some girl carrying a pot. She's kind of pretty, but messy, sort of long-haired with a skirt like a gypsy's, earth-motherish. Who's she?

"I thought you children might like something to eat," she says. She has one of those throaty voices. "It's chicken and herbs, the baby'll love it. I'm Nora. I live in the basement . . . Anytime you want to go out or anything, leave Jill with me, I adore children." She heads out and then calls over her shoulder, "Hammer on the floor if you need anything!"

I look at Sam. I mean, not that I'm the jealous type, but still! "Friend of yours?" I ask mockingly.

He just grins. "She lives downstairs, works in one of those psychedelic shops, I think . . . And on the third floor there's a family of Romanians with a trampoline . . . They run a gym or something. You're going to love it."

I feel so tired all of a sudden. I sit down on the bed. Wow, I hope I get some of my energy back. I really do want to do something around here, not just lie in bed all day. Maybe it's the excitement of it being the first day home.

Anyhow, Nora seemed nice. It'll be good to have someone in case we want to go out at night.

Sam looks worried, seeing me lying on the bed. "Want a glass of water?" he says.

I look at him and smile. "Just play me something."

He goes and gets his guitar. Jill lies next to me and we both listen. The sun is streaming in the window. I have a home again.

83

Part Two

In the chill of the damp night,
I ran silently and swiftly
to reach my destination,
thinking as I went,
of the despair and regret
we must face
at tomorrow's departure.
It is strange
that after so short a time
we must return to ourselves,
to our own minds
and decisions.
Why must we face this?
Why must we be forced down again
into the space
from which we've just emerged?
As I reach your door,

I hesitate.
Will this be the last time?
The last happiness we will know?
Perhaps years will pass,
and yet, we are forced to accept it,
for we are not yet old enough
for minds of our own.
Finally in your arms,
I realize,
this isn't the end!
It is only the beginning,
the youth of our love
and happiness.
Only our first departure.

I'm getting used to Vancouver, to living here, to the hospital. When I had the radiation I had to go every day, but that was only for a month or so. Now I just go in every couple of days for my shots. I'm getting to look like a junkie, my arms are all filled with needle jabs in my veins. My leg hurts, but I can forget about it a lot of the time and I'm used to the crutches.

Last week, we went to Sam's parents to pick up Jill. She stayed with them during the time when I was first out of the hospital, when I was getting my strength back. I hated going back to Riverdale to get her. I hated it because it hurt me to be reminded of when I was normal. It made me feel sorry for myself and I don't like that at all.

I like Sam's mother, but I also dislike her. She's so concerned about what people will think of her! She worries about the dumbest things. I almost can't take being around her at times.

Sam is so strong, so sure of his own thing. I love him so much. Last night he cried during the night for me. It's the first time he's let his emotions show, about my disease, so strongly. I felt close like we used to be, before all this happened. He is so wonderful. So much of a man. I love him.

Yes, I love thee
man
Yes, supply me with
hope
Yes, I love thee
man
You give me new life.

I'm writing my poems down now in a little notebook. I write them at night or when Jill's napping. I'd like to have a little book of poems to leave her, not just mine which aren't very good, I know, but ones by other people that mean something special to me.

In the end, after we stayed a weekend at Sam's parents, I felt I couldn't take it anymore, the strain was just too damn much. I don't hate Sam's parents, but they sure do make it hard not to. Thelma, his mother, still feels Sam is her little boy and incapable of taking care of himself. She thinks, since I married him, I am not capable of caring for either myself or Sam or, most of all, Jill. There are several things I have repeatedly asked her not to do with Jill, yet when I turn my back, she does them. She's this odd mixture of stupid strictness and spoiling. I don't think Jill likes it, it gets her all mixed up.

An example: Thelma is convinced Jill should be off her bottle now that she's over a year. I don't see why, and I told her the baby doctor said he didn't agree, that as long as she wasn't going to sleep sucking on the nipple which might do harm to her teeth, there's nothing wrong with a bottle. He even laughed, saying, "By the time she's married, no one will remember when she stopped her bottle." The time Jill usually wants her bottle is a very reasonable time, to me, around late afternoon, four or five, the time when it's not quite time to begin supper, but it's getting dark out. Lots of grown-ups have a drink then for the same reason. She'll keep on playing, with the bottle drooping out of her mouth so she can have her hands free. Or she'll set it beside her and now and then throw back her head and take a swig. What I like best are those times she comes to me and says she wants to lie in my lap. It comes out more like "yie in yap" since her l's aren't too clear. She lies down with her head in my lap, drinking her bottle. She keeps her eyes open and drinks seriously and steadily, taking the nipple out just to catch her breath. I stroke her hair which is finally growing in, so soft and fine, and we smile at each other. I see her mouth curve in a smile around her bottle and she holds on to my hand. I guess we must look like some pair of star-crossed lovers from a Hollywood musical. We don't talk at those times, but we're so close.

With Thelma, what bothers me is that because she helps us out financially, she feels she can do as she pleases. So when Jill asks for a bottle, she says, "Now big girls don't do that!" Sort of shaming her, which I hate. Or something like, "You must be a little baby, not a great big grown-up girl, to want a bottle!" Ugh! I've even asked her to stop giving us money, but she won't. What can I do? What is going to happen when I die? She's not going to have Jill, that's for sure. Sam will just have to understand that. She simply doesn't realize what's good for Jill and what isn't. Her argument is that she has already raised a son, but I don't know just how good a job she did. Right now I am totally mad at Sam and his faults are sticking out like a bad thumb. I love him, despite them. I respect him because he sticks up for them and hates me because I dislike them. But I won't change. His mom is too something or other—fucked up—to raise my daughter.

It's Sunday today, a day of rest. It's so beautiful. It must be fifty-five degrees, I can't believe it. Jill and I sat out on the step this morning. She didn't know what to do! She's just begun to be able to have some freedom outside and doesn't know which way to step first.

She and I have finally developed a good mother-daughter relationship. Since I got sick, things have been a little rough on her. For a while, after she was with Sam's parents, she was funny and awkward with me. Now she comes to me when she hurts or when strangers are about, and we have learned to communicate through touch and sounds that she makes. Everyone has told me, "When they get that age, watch out!" I don't understand. She minds well and is so inquisitive. I hope she is always that way. I'm so happy to see my child be healthy and happy and free and to not worry about a thing. She is a good child. Brag on, proud mama!

Friday, a boy I knew a little at the hospital, Jimmy—he had the same kind of cancer I do—died. He was sixteen. I felt so down, I can't even think about it. They had amputated his leg, but I guess it didn't help. I try not to think of him and suddenly, just while I'm sitting here with Jill or making supper, I think of it. I better try to pull out of it, I guess.

I have something to look forward to. This coming weekend, Pat, my little sister, is coming up to visit us! I'm so excited to see her again. I haven't seen her for four years. She was twelve then, a kid. Now she'll be grown-up. I bet Mom didn't want her to come. She still has this idea that Sam and I are living some wild, hippy existence here. If only she knew! Pat never had too much independence when she was little, but maybe she's changing now, I hope!

"Jill is so cute," Pat says. "She looks just like you, Kate!"

"Do you think so?" I feel so pleased I could burst. "I think she's more like David."

"Well, in coloring, maybe . . . But those big brown eyes, they remind me of you."

Pat is so pretty now, but she still has that sad quality she had when she was little. She's wearing contact lenses. She has that way of talking really low so you have to bend forward to hear her, and a sort of wistful expression. As kids we were close. She used to steal Mom's fall and wear it and tell everyone she was me.

I'm so glad she's come up. She's good for me. I feel a hundred times better since she came. When I heard about Jimmy, I guess it made me feel worse than I really thought I did. I had a sort of sick feeling all the time till Pat came. She's made me get into my old self again.

When Jimmy died, it seemed so cruel. It made me hate my disease with a new vigor. I can understand about myself, but not anyone else. I've learned a lot about life and love and happiness. I hope Jimmy did too, but most of all I hope his family did.

The other night, when I started thinking about dying, I had the most incredible melancholy feeling. I think that with the thought that I was dying and all, I began speeding a little, but I still felt this incredible calm. All the thoughts of what I should be doing, instead of lying there, were going so fast through my mind I couldn't keep up with them. I kept thinking: Let me have time to get everything done. I think I was almost pleading. There's so much I still have to do.

Sometimes, I wonder if I really accept that I am going to die. I thought so until I went to the conference with the doctors at the hospital the other day. They, of course, asked all these questions about death, and dying. How weird! And that always opens up all my thoughts on how I feel and I have to review them. I think I have accepted death, as well as anyone can, but what makes it hard is when I try to talk to people close to me and tell them what I'd like done—with Jill and Sam and my things. They refuse to listen and then I feel funny. It's such a hassle.

I can see all those questions in Pat's eyes, the way she looks at my crutches. She wants to know, but doesn't. I don't think I'll tell her. It would just be putting a burden on her and she's too young for that.

It's after supper and we're in the bedroom. We're going to a dance tonight with Sam and a friend of his, Gene.

"Isn't Jill sweet, really?" I say. "I mean, I know all mothers say that, but she's so good. They always say babies are so egotistical, that they can't think of other people, but she's not like that . . . If I'm tired, sometimes she'll go over and bring this blanket to me and tuck me in . . . I guess she likes pretending she's the mommy and I'm the baby. She'll offer me a drink from her bottle even . . . Or like with my crutches, sometimes she tries to walk on one leg like me. Or she'll cry when she sees the crutches, like she knows something is wrong."

Pat is frowning, looking at me with a worried expression. "Does she know anything is wrong?"

"No, not really . . . Maybe she senses a little. I'm sort of glad she's too young to—"

Pat is fiddling with something. "Are you used to the crutches?" she says.

"Oh sure . . . I don't think about them that much," I say. I know I'm not being honest.

"Does your leg hurt you a lot?"

"Sometimes . . . It's—well, what bothers me more is the medication they give me. It didn't seem to bother me at first, but lately I get so sick from it."

"You mean like throwing up?"

I nod. "Remember how we used to throw up when we were little and Mom always brought that basin so we wouldn't do it on the floor?"

Pat smiles. "I hated that, I hated throwing up."

"I guess maybe it'll pass, this thing of feeling queasy . . . I hope it does."

"You look nice," she says eagerly.

"Yeah, well, at least I'm not fat anymore . . . You should have seen me right after Jill was born. I was a hippo!"

"I can't imagine it . . . You?"

"Really . . . I just ate and ate. Peanut brittle and lollipops, pizza, everything . . . If I had another baby, I'd never—" I stop. What's wrong with me? I'm not going to have another baby.

Pat is looking at herself in the mirror with that careful, critical look of a sixteen-year-old, wanting, praying she'll pass muster. "What do you think about my hair?" she says.

"It's really pretty, Pat . . . It looks nice long."

"Hey girls!" Sam calls. "Aren't you ready yet?"

"Just a sec!" I yell. I like sitting in the bedroom with Pat. It's like the old days.

"Sam is nice," Pat says, sort of shyly.

"Isn't he great? He really is the way he seems. He—" Oh, it's impossible to talk about someone you love. Either it sounds like boasting or as if you're making it up.

"I think he's better for you than David was," Pat says. She giggles. "I was always sort of scared of David."

"Yeah, he was like that." Gosh, David seems so long ago. "I saw him a few months ago."

"Did you? How come?"

"Oh, he tried to pull this thing . . . He said he wanted Jill."

"How could he? She's your baby!"

"I know . . . Only she's his too, technically . . . He didn't want her, it was just to spite me. He said I was too young to be a good mother, all that stuff."

"*I* think you're a wonderful mother," Pat says. "If I ever have a baby I want to be just like you."

No one is like Pat. No one ever just plain admired me the way she does. It makes me feel so good. I can't help saying, "I wish Mom would come see Jill, though . . . I mean, how come she doesn't even care? It's her own grandchild." Oh, quiet, Kate. I know the answer to that, but it just spilled out.

Pat looks embarrassed. She doesn't want to bad-mouth about Mom but she's on my side too which makes it hard for her. "Well, she . . ."

"No, I know," I say bitterly. "I'm her wild, hippy daughter who's living in rags and smoking pot all the time and . . . But if she'd only come up and see! She'd see all that wasn't true! You'll tell her, won't you?"

"Sure," Pat says quickly. But Pat is so meek and gentle. Nothing she says will influence Mom. Somehow, Mom will just think I brainwashed her.

We drive to the dance. Sam is all dressed up in his flowered shirt and looks great. I like Gene, though I don't know him too well. He's small, not much taller than Pat with a kind of scraggly black moustache and wire glasses. I think he likes Pat, which pleases me.

Of course I can't dance! It isn't that I thought I could, but sitting here for three hours watching is more depressing than I thought it would be. It's not just jealousy. I like Sam to dance, I like watching him. I know he loves me, but I know he likes women and he's

98

appealing to them. He ought to dance, it's good for him. And I like watching Pat too. But at the same time it really makes me hurt, makes me want to cry. I don't think that's silly. I love to dance and I think it's a shame that I can't. Damn damn damn! Well, I guess I'll have to find a way to cope. What I hate is when I have to get up to go to the toilet, and all these guys make smart remarks. I just tell them I got hit by a car. That shuts them up. It's not that I'm bitter. If someone asks nicely and with genuine feeling, not with just a desire to hear the gory details, then I tell them the truth. But I hate those dudes that aren't considerate enough to even get out of my way until I've given them a bunch of shit. Gets to be such a drag and it makes me even more self-conscious.

Pat's still here. She'll stay one more day. I'm loving having her, it's like a birthday and Christmas present rolled into one. She's so nice with Jill. If only she weren't so young, then maybe she could be someone to think of to look after Jill when I die.

Tonight they're going to the dance without me. They just left. I guess I'm a coward. I couldn't face it again. That and I felt tired. It's raining out, a good time to curl up in bed and listen to music on the radio, maybe write something in my notebook. They're playing some good stuff, oldies but goodies. Wish they'd play "Sweet Little Sheila."

Nightime is overtaking me
as daylight falls behind.
My life is slowly losing
the sparkle and the shine.

100

A life filled with promises
and empty bottles of wine.
This loneliness is beginning to
encloak me,
I've lost all sense of time.
Self-pity overwhelms me,
I've begun to lose my mind.
While death is overtaking me
and daylight falls behind.

Sometimes I think I'm very much afraid to be alone.
Knowing that I will die makes me want all the life right
now that I can get. I don't want to be alone yet.

Being alone in the apartment at night is a little
spooky. I'm glad Jill is here. Even if she's asleep, just
having her here makes me feel better. I could go down
and ask Nora to come up and keep me company. But I
don't really like her so much. Ironically, I feel about her
what Mom probably feels about me—that she's messy
and her life seems haphazard, with no real plan. She
knows all the things she doesn't like—she's real down on
her family, much worse than me!—but it seems like
there isn't so much positive she does like. To me she
seems aimless. I don't care if someone works or doesn't
work or has a child or doesn't, those are personal
decisions, but I do feel people should have something,
some center. I see these guys coming to see her and they
look grimy. There's no love there, just sleeping around.
Wow, I sound like some little old lady. Sermon of the
day. Well, I do feel like that, I'm sorry. Maybe being a
mama has made me too critical.

When I'm alone like this, every little noise sounds so
loud! I hope I'm not getting paranoid.

One thing that's scaring me tonight is that we supposedly have a ghost in the house! All the tenants have heard him and we all thought it was one or the other of us pounding, but then we found it really wasn't any of us! Sam says it's all garbage. He admits there's a noise and he isn't sure what it is, but he's sure it's just some squeaky thing with the house, which is pretty old. I don't know. Mrs. Schaeffer, who lives upstairs, told me she thought it was her husband trying to contact her—he died last year. Maybe it's my future ghost calling me to join him! (her!). Oh lordy. I think one does tend to get carried away about such matters. But then, who knows? Perhaps such things do for a fact exist.

"Mommy!" It's Jill. I can't tell if she's asleep or awake. Sometimes she calls out in her sleep.

"What is it, puss?"

She stands up sleepily in her crib. "Morning?"

"No, it's not morning . . . It's nighttime. See how dark it is out."

"Dark," she says, looking around. "Daddy?"

"No, Daddy's not here . . . He went to a dance with Aunt Pat . . . Are you hungry? Would you like a little snack?" I must confess I'm glad she's up. Now I'll have company.

"Jill hungry," she says.

"Okay, let me lift you out."

We decide on bowls of chocolate chip ice cream and some Oreos as a snack. She sits next to me on the couch, munching, clearly very pleased to be up. She sees Sam's guitar on the bed. "Mommy play?"

102

"No, Mommy can't play, darling . . . I don't know how."

"Daddy play?"

"Yes, Daddy can play, he's very good."

"Daddy play now?"

"No, Daddy can't play now. He's not here. He's at the dance."

"Dance?"

"You know . . . Jill can dance." I get up and imitate dancing as best I can on one foot.

Jill smiles, delighted. "More dance, Mommy!"

"Well, Mommy's not too good at dancing anymore, puss . . . You dance, Jill dance."

She gets up and stumbles around, trying her best, then falls into my lap, giggling. "Puss, you better get back to sleep . . . It's late. It's a long time till morning."

"Mommy sleep?"

"Yes, Mommy will sleep too." I glance at the clock. It's past eleven. I do feel tired. I tuck Jill in her crib and then go and lie down. I see her peeking at me from behind the rails of her crib. "Good night, puss."

" 'Night, Mommy."

Soon she is snoring. She sleeps so heavily. I wish I could. Dr. Gillman gave me some pain pills for when my leg bothers me at night, but I hate to take them. They make me so groggy. Anyway, I'd like to be awake when the others get home. But when will that be? Maybe quite late. I lie there, seeing Sam in my mind, dancing.

I do fall asleep, but when they come in I hear them. They must have stopped at the bar again—Sam's breath, as he kisses me, smells of beer. But it's a good smell. I don't mind. Because Pat is here we won't make love, but Sam holds me and that's good enough.

"Was it fun?" I whisper.

"Sort of . . . We missed you."

"Jill woke up . . . but it was nothing. She was just hungry."

"Did the ghost put in an appearance?"

"Come on!"

"Did you have Nora come up?"

"No, I didn't feel like it."

"I just thought you'd like company."

"Umm." I feel petty telling Sam how I feel about Nora so I just say, "I didn't feel lonely . . . I listened to the radio and stuff."

He's stroking my hair. "Sleep tight, sweetheart."

"You too."

Three in the morning. Soon it'll be light. Tomorrow Pat will go home. I'll go to the hospital.

It would be so good if Sam could get a job, a real job, something connected with music that he could really love. Since my illness he's picked up odd jobs here and there, enough so we can scrape by financially without having to mooch too much off his parents. Right now he's bartending at O'Brien's most evenings. But I think having to take that kind of job again bothers him. It's just marking time, and he must feel, as I do, that if it weren't for my illness, maybe I could pull my share somewhat more.

I have to go to the hospital this afternoon. I dread it. The medication is making me so sick. I never feel right anymore. In the couple of months since Pat visited it seems like there hasn't been a day when I haven't thrown up. It's not just that, I feel so—distant, in a fog, like I'm not a real person. It scares the hell out of me.

I can't seem to break out of myself. For days now my

thought process has been so dull and I don't know why. I just can't seem to think intelligently. It's really bothering me. Maybe it's the way Sam and I have been living. We're so unaware of what's going on around us. We never read or discuss situations anymore. We just end up arguing about things because we're both too poorly informed to discuss anything. This is a real problem. I think we should do something about it. I think a trip to the library is definitely in order. I've been wanting to go for several days now, but like so many other things we want to do, it hasn't been done. Why? I guess until now it hasn't bothered me quite this much. I wish I could get a job so that I could be out with people. Seclusion is no good at all. I need fresh ideas and new thoughts. My mind has simply used up all of its resources and I have failed to feed it. I think I'll buy some books and put myself on a new diet.

Jill is sleeping. She seems so fussy lately, whining about everything, sucking her thumb. That bothers me too. What can I do?

I'm sitting in the bedroom listening to Sam and Weaver practice. I just wrote an angry poem. Here it is. It's called America Hurrah, Ha, Ha, Ha:

You may take your poverty aid,
and your military aid,
and your foreign aid,
and even your cool aid,
for what it's worth,
america.

You may burn us for
burning our draft cards,

(as our mothers once
burned us before, for
playing with matches)
but it no longer matters,
america.

You can prosecute us,
for not killing in an unjust war,
for wanting peace,
through a universal, workable understanding,
love.

I don't want to kill a person, for such an unworthy
cause,
as we are fighting for now.

I DEFY YOU AMERICA!

You can imprison us for years,
and months
of young and productive lives
because we happen to have the guts,
america,
the *guts*,
to stand for what we believe in,
because we are human;
because we retain our humanity,
despite your propaganda.

You can stifle the lives
of those who haven't been told
but not me,
america. I—
I'm free, you hear!
They only can understand
as far as you have taught them
(and that's not very far).

Their minds have grown lethargic and old.
Freedom can't be won with a song.

Right! It takes many voices
and many songs.
We! We are the ones that matter!
You have grown old
and have done your work.

Let us grow old as we wish.
Step aside.

I prefer the feel of a newborn child,
and a man's hand on my shoulder
to that of a weapon,
whether material
or immaterial.

I told you I was in a bad mood! Yeah, it's no good, I
know that too. I listen to Sam and Weaver. They have
their music. However good it really is, it's something,
their own. It seems I never accomplish anything. I feel
so utterly worthless. A poorly written book of poetry
that *no one* will want to read. Even if I *hit* them! I need
to accomplish something and be good at it and be
praised for it. I need an outer source of expression. Sam
always ignores this. When I ask him to read something
I've just written, he puts it off till later. I never am able
to get involved in something. There's always something
to do—Sam to feed, Jill to take care of, the hospital to
go to, cancer in the back of my mind, hatred for all the
things I am not. And Weaver. Always the fear that he or
his music will take Sam away from me.

Why did Weaver come up here? And when is he

going to leave? God, I hate a moocher! He's just staying on, thinking we don't mind if he eats our food. Sam had to be an idiot and say that three can eat as cheaply as one. Not when one of them is Weaver!

I guess I should get going now. See you later, folks! Want to bet Weaver is still here when I get back?

The hospital is my second home. I know it so well by now, I know every nurse, every doctor, a lot of the other kids. I don't mind the hospital itself, or the treatments. It's not even the thought of dying I mind the most. Dying is beautiful, even the first time around, at the ripe old age of twenty. It's not easy most of the time, but there is a real beauty to be found in knowing that your end is going to catch up with you faster than you had expected and that you have to get all your loving and laughing and crying done as soon as you can. You know you don't have time to play games. You don't want to waste precious moments doing nothing or feeling nothing.

That's why I mind the medications—because they make the time I do have, however long it may be, meaningless. I want so much to make someone understand that. Each time I come here, I decide I will finally tell Dr. Gillman how I feel. Then I lose courage, knowing she'll be angry with me. But it's *my* life!

When I get out of the hospital, it's raining. Weaver seems to have gone home. Jill is in the kitchen, but I don't have time even to say hi to her. I just rush into the bathroom and vomit into the toilet. I make a wonderful entrance every day like this. Sam is playing his guitar, I'm throwing up. What a great scene. True love.

I lie down on the bed. Oh, I feel so bitter, so down, I can't even fight it. Finally I say, "How can you sing when I'm throwing up?"

"How can you throw up when I'm singing?" Sam says.

"The pills make me throw up!" I scream. "I can't help it. You *know* that."

"The Christians sang when they were thrown to the lions." He smiles. "It just seemed like a good thing to do, in the face of adversity."

I laugh, bitter. I can taste the bitter, sour taste in my mouth from throwing up. As a kid, I liked throwing up because afterward I felt better and I'd eat a bowl of applesauce. Now I feel the same after as before.

Sam gets up and sits on the bed next to me. He touches my hair. I jerk away. I don't want him, I don't want anyone. Shoot me like an old horse. It's better than this. This is torture. "Kate," he says.

"I can't keep my food down," I say, "I can't sleep, my hair is coming out in handfuls and you want me to laugh at your sick jokes . . . I *am* a sick joke."

"Then laugh at yourself."

"I can't!"

"It's better than crying."

111

I get up. "I'm *not* crying!"

"Baby—"

"They can't even find a vein that's any good anymore to put the shots in. They're going to have to put it in my temple next time. Oh, it's a riot. A laugh a minute." I go into the kitchen and there's Jill, in the middle of the most incredible mess. She's gotten out this bottle of ketchup and has smeared it on everything—herself, the wall, the floor. Can't Sam keep an eye on her for one second and put down that damned guitar!

"What are you doing!" I scream, snatching the ketchup bottle from her. "You know better than that. That's bad. You're a bad, bad girl!" I yank her off the kitchen table, but Sam comes in and grabs her away from me. His face! Like I'm going to kill her. I'm her *mother!*

Jill breaks loose and runs into the next room.

"Sam—"

"Let me get Jill," he says curtly.

"Talk to *me!*"

He pulls away, angry. "In a minute!"

He goes off after her and takes her into the bathroom. I can hear the water running. He must be washing her off. I can't help it. I go to the rocker and cry. It's all going, everything I love, I'm killing it. I'm destroying Jill and Sam. There's nothing left. I'm becoming a monster.

Sam comes in with Jill. Now she looks mad, but he looks calm.

"Why don't we go out to the park?" Sam says.

"It's raining."

"It's stopped . . . Look."

"Park! Park!" Jill says, excited.

I look at her, her rumpled hair. My baby. "Come give Mommy a kiss first," I say. "To cheer her up . . . Okay?"

Jill looks at me evenly, as though considering the proposition. Then, "No!" she says stubbornly and loudly. She runs to the door.

"Kate, come on," Sam says. "Come with us."

"I'm not going to any stupid park with a child who hates me."

"She doesn't hate you."

"I'm not going to compete with you for my baby!"

"Nobody's competing."

"She's mine, Sam. Remember? Not yours. You're stealing her from me. The only thing in the world that's altogether mine. I know what you're doing—"

His face is cold, angry again. "Sure, I'm taking care of another man's kid twenty-four hours a day just out of spite. I have nothing else to do."

"You don't have a job."

"How will I get a job if I'm a full-time baby-sitter?"

"Then leave her! Leave us! Who said you should do it!"

"I love her. I do it because I love her . . . And I love you when you act like yourself."

"This is myself."

"It's not." He turns and takes Jill's hand.

I call after them, "You're teaching her to hate me so that when I die she won't be so much trouble. You can marry any old broad. Anyone'll be better than mean old Mommy who—"

They're gone. Oh God, maybe they won't come back. I feel like I'm at the bottom of a well. I can't see, I can't

113

hear, I can't move. If Jill turns against me, that's the end. That matters so much to me, loving her, having her love me. If she ever felt about me the way I got to feel about Mom, I would truly die. I know one reason Mom never liked me was because Dad did, I was his favorite. He used to kind of flirt with me and whirl me around and she'd get this real angry, hostile expression. Or if he took me out, just to the zoo or to the candy store, anything, she'd get a sick headache and have to go to bed. If they had a fight, she'd say to me sarcastically, "You ask your father. For you, he'll do it." It wasn't my fault! I didn't make him like me! But I knew she held it against me.

If Jill feels that way—oh God. I'm not jealous of her that way. Sam and I have something good together. I would like nothing better than if she, when she grows up, finds someone as good as Sam. But lately, I feel I have no patience with her. I don't care about the ketchup. So what? So she spills it! It can be cleaned up in a second. I know that. I even like her to mess around, I want her to, I want her to get dirty and play in the mud. I never want her to be dressed up in some pink, ruffly dress and then spanked because she got it dirty. Let her wear overalls if she's more comfortable in them . . . But I just don't have any patience. What's happened? I just snap like a string.

Maybe I am jealous of both of them. Of Sam for having his music. Even if he doesn't have a job, he has a center to his life, something he's good at, something he loves, something that brings him in contact with others . . . And I feel jealous of Jill because—well, this sounds ironic now—but because she has the freedom I never

114

did, she has parents who let her do what she wants. She'll be strong when she grows up. Maybe I mind that she's too young to know about my sickness. Really, I'm glad. Because why should she have that? It would just be a burden. It would be worse, much worse if she was just old enough to understand, but not to really understand. I feel that, but at times she seems so heartless not to know, to go on doing her own baby things while I'm throwing up and my leg is hurting. For all she knows, that's what all mommies do. All mommies throw up every day. That's just their thing.

I shouldn't have blamed Sam for not looking after Jill well enough. He does it so well, better than me, he's so much more patient. And I'm not even sure that's just because he's not sick, I think he really is good with kids, really senses their moods very well . . . Of course, he can't watch her every second. He does have to practice. How will he get good enough to audition otherwise? . . . Anyway, I don't watch Jill every second I'm with her. You'd go crazy if you did that.

Should I go after them? Where did they go, even? There's one park near here. That's where they probably went. Jill likes it because it has this funny climbing thing in the middle painted with all different colors. And it has two slides, a little one for small children and a big one for big children. I usually take her there a few times a week.

Okay, I'll go there. I still feel sick, but maybe getting out would be good.

There they are. I see Sam standing near the bottom of the slide. Jill is at the top, just sitting there, kicking her legs, building up the suspense of when she'll slide down. I stand a minute watching them. Then I go down the hill. I walk slowly over to Sam, my crutch under my arm. "Hi."

He turns. "Hi," he says. He doesn't smile.

"I figured I could use some air."

He just nods, abstracted.

Jill sees me and waves. "Hi, Mommy!"

Jesus, children forget so fast! "Hi, honey! . . . Are you sliding down?"

I see another child climbing up behind her. "I'm at the top," she says.

"I see, that's great . . . Are you going to come down?"

Finally, reluctantly, feeling the impatient breath of the next child, she lets go and slides to the bottom. Then she races over to the climbing thing and crawls in. It's filthy and wet from the rain. Okay, let it go. She'll have a bath when she gets home anyway.

"I feel so bad when we fight like that," Sam says.

"I know." I take his hand. It's cold.

"Especially in front of Jill."

"Kids are tougher than we are," I say flippantly.

"I don't know about that."

"She's forgotten already . . . Look at her!" Jill is peeking out of the holes in the climbing bar. She waves at us.

"Should Daddy lift you down?" Sam asks.

"No!" Jill says indignantly. "Do it *myself!*"

He laughs. "Everything is 'do it myself' lately, I guess."

I seem to see us from a distance. A couple holding hands, a pretty little girl, married less than a year,

116

happiness . . . Tomorrow I will go into the hospital and Dr. Gillman will say: There's a new drug, just discovered, with amazing results. No side effects . . . Yeah sure.

Jill climbs down and falls on her bottom, but pulls herself up again. She loves being out of doors. On cold, rainy days she'll stand by the door looking out sadly. You've forgotten me, haven't you, puss?

"Maybe we better get back . . . Jill can have her bath. I got some bubble stuff for her."

"Okay." Sam still seems distant, a little detached. I know our arguing takes a lot out of him also, and that makes me feel bad.

As we're walking off, two men come into the playground with two dogs. Mongrels, probably, but nice-looking ones. They both go right over to the slide—the dogs, that is—climb up the steps and slide down. Jill lets out a delighted laugh. "Did you see, Mommy?"

"Yes . . . Isn't that amazing?"

Then the dogs, on command, leap over the fence surrounding the swings. I watch Jill's face. Will she remember that years from now? I was in the playground with my mommy and daddy and two dogs went down a slide? Or is she too young? Will all this fade? I can't remember anything from when I was her age. That seems so strange, that one would remember nothing. But that's the way it is, I guess. I pray I live long enough to see Jill become a human being independent of Sam and me. At least old enough to reason some on her own. Old enough so she'll remember me.

"We can pick up a pizza on the way home," Sam says. He has his arm around my shoulder, more relaxed again.

"I want a horsie ride!" Jill calls impatiently and he bends down and scoops her up high onto his shoulders. "I'm bigger than you, Mommy."

"I see, puss." The other day Jill and I were playing with two cats, one the mother, the other, now full-grown, the son. I began explaining how one day she would be bigger than me, just like the cat was now bigger than his mother. She seemed to be listening very carefully and then at the end she said, "When I grow up, I will be a pussycat." I said, "No, when you grow up, you'll be a big woman, like Mommy," but that didn't please her at all. She insisted that she was going to be a pussycat and nothing I could say would dissuade her.

Jill likes to watch me put on my makeup. "Me ma" she calls it, "Mommy's me ma." It's funny. Before I got sick I hardly wore any—oh, maybe some eye makeup when I wanted to look good because I think my eyes are my best feature. But since I've been sick, I've been wearing lipstick and rouge just so I won't look so pale and wretched. Sam put these photos up in the bathroom. There's one of me before I got sick. I was so much heavier in the cheeks—now my bones are very hollow. I'm very photogenic now, like a model. But to me it's the same face. I see in it the spark of laughter that made me such a happy child and the traces of wisdom that made me a mother. I see the pain and beauty of childbirth, the agony of loss of health, the peace from trying to gain freedom over all of it. I see a woman. I don't look like a girl anymore. I see a few

119

lines, lines of struggle, lines on my nineteen-year-old face—a map of pain and sorrow and joy and happiness, and perhaps, at my eyes and mouth, peace in knowing who I am."

"Put lipstick on me, Mommy," Jill says. She purses her lips and I stroke them gently with the tip of the lipstick.

"Put rouge on me." You don't need rouge, you silly. She looks funny with rouge. She won't let me blend it in so it's just two red streaks on her fat cheeks.

Jill's getting pretty. I can tell by the way people look at her and smile. I'm glad. I wouldn't want her to be spectacularly beautiful, like a movie actress, but I think being pretty, nice-looking, makes things easier. She's a baby still, but she's so much into things, so much a part of every moment. She loves to play dress up, draping these old scarves and things around her. Sometimes she'll put on ten at once, like an old gypsy fortune-teller. She gets mad when they fall off. When I clean house, she goes around copying me, pretending to dust. In the car she sticks her head out the window and sings to the wind and the passing cars. She only knows one song, "Oh, we're going in the car, oh, we're going in the train, oh, we're going in the boat . . ." It can go on forever, like a chant. Sometimes she tries to walk on one leg like I do. What will she be like when she grows up? Maybe she'll be tall and willowy and sing sad songs or maybe, more likely, she'll be giving songs to people from her heart instead of just singing sad ones.

"Mommy has to go now, puss," I say, having done the best I can with my face.

"Jill go too?"

"No, Jill will stay with Nora . . . Mommy will be back soon and then we'll go to the park."

I know Jill doesn't like staying with Nora. I pray that today she goes off without a fuss. It wears me down so to leave after a huge battle. What else can I do?

"Mommy will see you later," I say as Nora comes out to greet us.

"Don't go, Mommy!" Jill says suddenly. She comes running to me, clutching me around the knees.

"Darling, I have to, I have to go to the hospital."

"Take me . . . I want to go too."

"I can't take you . . . They don't allow little girls."

"Let's play your game, Jill," Nora says in a cheerful voice. She says once I leave Jill's okay.

"No!" Jill yells. "Mommy will stay!"

I yank away from her. "Jill, stop it!" I hear my voice, too shrill, on the verge of hysteria. "Leave me alone!"

"Just go!" Nora says. She holds Jill back by force. Jill's face is red from screaming. She looks like she's going to have a heart attack.

I dash away, not daring to look at them. Oh God, I hate this! Why can't Sam be here when I leave? Once I'm out of sight, my heart still pounding too fast, I wish I hadn't gotten hysterical. I can't help it, lately. I feel myself getting out of control, but I can't stop it. It's awful.

I'm going to tell Dr. Gillman today to take me off the drugs and the radiation. Every night I've been preparing what I'll say to her. It's so important to me that she understand, understand what they've been doing to me. I trust her, more than any of the other doctors. For some of them I think a patient is just a guinea pig. They

121

want to try the medication just to see "how it works." They've trained themselves not to think of their patients as human beings. I can understand that. It must be hard to become attached to people and then have them just die on you. But I think it's so much more important that they consider each patient, how the medication is affecting them. They do these tests on monkeys, or whatever, and then try them out on their patients, not seeming to care that we're not monkeys. That sounds silly to even have to think, but there are many times when I don't think they make any distinction. We're like laboratory animals.

As far as I'm concerned, they can take their egos and go sit on them. My life is important to me and if I'm only going to live a short time, then, that's cool, but I'm going to live it to the fullest.

It's so easy to say this to myself, it all seems so perfectly clear and understandable, but as I try to explain it to Dr. Gillman, I feel myself getting stubborn and defensive, afraid she's going to get angry at me. I need her approval, which is childish, I know.

"You don't feel you want to try it a few months more?" she says.

"I've tried it! I've been on it six months! . . . Why are you such an egotist?"

She smiles. "In what way am I an egotist?"

"Because if you weren't, you'd see how I feel! You'd say—okay, we tried to help you with these drugs, but if you feel you're unable to take them, then we want to understand why. You'd see that a person's mind is just as important as their body in getting well . . . Maybe for some people the drugs are fine, but you'd say—Kate isn't 'some people'—she's a particular person."

"I *do* want to understand, Kate. Believe me, I do."

"Then understand!"

"It's a matter of prolonging your life—"

"I'm not *alive!* That's what I'm trying to say. With these drugs I don't even want to live. I've lost the will to live, to care for my family. I'm too emotionally upset to look after Jill. I don't pay attention to anything but my own self-pity or sorrow. It's horrible!"

Dr. Gillman brings a chair and sits down next to me. She takes my hand in hers. I can tell by her touch that she understands and that makes me so relieved I want to cry. But I can't, I can't talk even. I just sit, so glad for her warmth. Finally, I look up at her. "You ought to find yourself a man and have about two hundred children . . . You'd be the world's greatest mother."

"I have three hundred and fifty children right here . . . You're my oldest."

I look at her, mocking. "And your most difficult?"

"Right now."

There's a long silence. I don't think she did understand, only that I hurt and she senses that. I can tell she still thinks I'm acting like a child, not obeying what she says will be good for me. "I'll give you Jill," I say.

She looks startled. "What do you mean?"

"Either take me off all this stuff—the shots, the pills, the radiation . . . or take Jill. Because it's not fair to her to have a mother who acts the way I do when I'm on this stuff. I can't do it to her."

"That's a bit extreme, don't you think?"

"Look, I could go on with it, maybe, if it just meant throwing up three times a day and flushing my hair out in tufts every day. I'm even getting used to looking like a piece of spaghetti . . . But I'll never get used to what I'm doing to Sam and Jill."

"Sam understands, though, doesn't he?"

"Maybe, some . . . but Jill doesn't. She *can't!* All she knows is that her mommy is screaming at her twenty-five hours a day . . . She never used to cry at all. She didn't have any reason to. She was happy. Now she cries all the time. She cries in her sleep. She wakes up crying. She has nightmares. She chews her fingers. If I come to her in the night, she screams . . . The only thing I ever really wanted to do is to have a child, a girl, and raise her like I should've been raised. With nothing but love and freedom. With no fancy clothes and stiff shoes, no Puritan ethic, no rules, no right answers to everything. So she could be open to the sun and snow and rocks and rain and know how to love. It's terribly hard when you've never been loved. When all you've ever known is people screaming at you and telling you you're bad."

My voice is getting shaky, but I feel I've said it all and if she doesn't understand now, she never will.

"If you go off the medication, you will die," Dr. Gillman says.

"I'm going to die anyway."

She hesitates. "Probably, yes."

"So, don't you see, I'd much rather die peacefully with some semblance of sanity than take the drugs and die a bit later than I might have naturally with no mind at all . . . That's what's happening to me. I'm losing my mind."

124

"I see."

"Do you really? . . . I mean, tell me if you don't."

"I do."

"Will the other doctors? . . . Will I have to go through this again with them? I'm not sure I can."

"I'll speak to them."

I feel wiped out. I can tell my body is wet with sweat under my turtleneck.

"I think Jill is lucky to have a mother who cares that much about relating to her."

I wince a little. "I don't know. I wonder if she's lucky . . . Sometimes I think—it's so hard for all of us . . . There's so much I would've liked to tell her, do with her, and she's just too young! I can't."

"Have you ever thought of writing it down?"

"Oh, I do . . . poems and things. But I'm not a good poet."

"Well, why don't you write prose, then? Just all those things you were mentioning that you'd like to tell her about?"

"Well . . . I don't know. I don't know if I can . . . Where would I start?"

"Anticipate her questions . . . When she's six, what you'd say to her. What she's going to want to know."

"Nothing." I laugh. "By the time you're six, you know everything."

"Then—when she's ten or sixteen, whatever."

I try to think about it. Jill at ten, at sixteen.

"About boys, your feeling for nature, love . . . so she'll know you and how you feel about her."

"But the trouble is, I can't type and writing takes so long . . . Somehow when I sit down with a sheet of

125

paper in front of me, I get all tight. I'm that way with letters even. It seems so—I don't know, final, to write it down."

"Why not tape it, then?"

"What do I buy a tape recorder with? Food stamps?"

Dr. Gillman opens her bottom drawer and takes out a tape recorder. It's marked: "Property of children's hospital. Do not remove." She puts some tapes down next to it. "How about it?"

"Can I take it home with me?"

"Sure, that's the point."

"But it belongs to the hospital."

"That's *my* problem."

I stare at it, fascinated. "Will it be hard to learn how to work it?"

"Not at all . . . You know, I brought it up because I'm like you, Kate. I get all stiff when I face a piece of paper. So whenever I have a speech or something to deliver, I just speak it into here. Somehow talking is much easier, less official . . . And what's great is you can erase whatever you don't like. It's really simple to work."

I take the tape recorder and tapes in my lap. I love you, Dr. Gillman, I think, but I can't quite bring myself to say it aloud. I'm sure she knows. She knows everything.

"Kate, I'm not trying to revert to our earlier topic, but—"

"Yes?" I steel myself.

"Well, there is a new drug, one we haven't tried on you yet . . . What would you say to trying it just for a short time? . . . If it has the same effect as the others, then we'll discontinue it."

"Has it been tested yet?"

"The experiments are still running. They've been going two years."

"Is it a depressant?"

"No, but—"

"Does it make you throw up?"

"It doesn't make monkeys throw up."

"Wonderful."

"What do you say then?"

"I don't know . . ."

"It's a long shot. I won't lie to you."

"Do you promise that if I come back to you and say it has the same effect as the other drugs you'll take me off it, no questions asked?"

"I promise."

"Cross your heart and hope to die?"

"Kate!" She laughs.

"I wish you'd been my mother," I blurt out.

"Then you wouldn't have been you."

"True . . . but think how great I would have been, how secure . . . *Will* you have a baby one day?"

Her face gets sad. "I don't know . . . I'm so involved in my work, I'm not sure it would be fair."

I can see that. "I hope sometime you do, though . . . because I think you'd love it."

She smiles. Her expression is much softer, more vulnerable than usual. "I hope I will someday."

I go home excited but peaceful. So glad she understood. That in itself makes me very happy . . . But most of all, I'm so excited about having the tape recorder. I want so much, in what time there is left to me, to leave something for Jill, some record on these tapes that later Sam could have typed into a book. Some part of me. I want to tell her about how I feel. About how I did things. About how important she is to me. Now she's too young to understand. But later, when I'm not around, she'd have something to come to, she could hear my voice, listen. I have so many things to tell about, it's hard to know where to begin!

The earliest thing I can remember was when my mother took us to the zoo for the first time and we were feeding the elephants. I ran out of peanuts and popcorn so I grabbed my white sandals off my feet and threw them in. My sisters thought it was a great idea and wanted to throw in more clothes, but Mom caught us before we could strip down. I may think that was the beginning, but I bet Mom thought it was the beginning of the end. I was four then. How I hated those damn sandals!

I remember my mother then. I thought she was the most beautiful mommy in the world. I loved the way she smelled, the way she wore her black hair, the proud way she carried herself. When we walked down the streets of town, even with four grubby little girls clinging to her skirts, all the men looked, and I wanted to be just like that. And I was. I knew it because men started falling in love with me when I was only eleven. They saw in me the same fire and beauty that was in her.

There were things I didn't understand about my mom and dad. I still don't. They had bad fights. I remember some Christmases he wasn't there. Did he have other women? I don't know. Once there was a fight and he stormed out. Mom was crying and I came and took her in my arms; I must have been twelve or so. I told her I would always take care of her. We held each other so tight! That was one time we loved each other freely without all the bad things, the tension that I always felt between us . . . They had other fights too. One time the six of us went for a ride in the mountains. We had a brand-new Oldsmobile, one of those long black and white ones. They could go ninety miles an hour and so could my dad. He and Mom got in a fight just as we came to what is known as Five Mile Hill up the Poudre Canyon in Colorado. Dad started up the hill as fast as he could go just to scare Mom. I know he must have been going sixty-five at the time, and that's a lot on a little dirt road. We girls sat in the back scared stiff, our feet straight out in front of us, and heads back against the seat, fervently praying. But Daddy was a good driver and we made it to the top of the hill!

I know one thing Mom holds against me is the time I got drunk with Henry McDoughall just before I went off and married David. I was just scared about getting married, that was all. Maybe it was my way of showing her I was scared, wanting her to understand and sympathize. I never drank outside of that time. I really can't stand liquor or beer to this day. I never smoked

130

either, not even grass that much because Mom taught me how to get high when she taught me the names of mountain flowers and when she taught me to speak up for myself and when she taught me how to love, when she gave me my first dog. She taught me living was beautiful and I believed her because she was beautiful and knew how to share it. If only I could understand why things got bad between us!

I can't remember too much of school. There were all those games: red rover, red rover, let Kate come over. I didn't like that game. I could never get through and I always got sent back and then no one on my side would let me play again. I had a friend in first grade. Her name was Alice. We pretended to be sisters. Everyone thought we were a little crazy, but we didn't care. We would hide in the top of the fire-escape tunnel and whisper stories about our parents to each other. I told her how, after we went to bed, my dad and mom would sit up and drink beer and kiss and stuff. She said her parents did too.

One day in the lunchroom a little kid bit into a piece of pizza and got a straight pin stuck in his mouth. He screamed and everyone got scared. I went to the girl's lavatory (as we were instructed to call it) and threw up. Mom let me take my lunch to school after that.

On shot days I'd try to be sick and stay home, but Mom knew my tricks and sent me to school anyway. I used to have visions of the needle breaking off in my arm and traveling around in my body until it finally stabbed me in the heart, causing my death. People would come to my funeral and mourn. The school nurses would be thrown out of town and shots would be abolished . . . I had asthma too, and was allergic to goldenrod, so that meant more shots. A lovely summer day, sneeze, sneeze. The next thing I knew I'd be in the doctor's office getting shots for asthma. Tall white walls, stainless-steel medicine chest, stainless-steel nurses. Count to ten, dearie, you won't feel a thing. 1 2 3 Mama, are you still there? 4 5 Please, lady, don't let it hurt. 6—jab! Screams would erupt from my body like volcanic explosions. Mama, let's go home and not come here anymore.

We never got an allowance. There just wasn't any extra money to go around, especially with the four of us. If I wanted to earn money, I'd pick pine cones. There was a woman in a nearby village who made Christmas wreaths for people. I gathered the pine cones to put on those wreaths. Eventually, I graduated to tying the wreaths and then to decorating them. But the first thing I did was gather pine cones.

You got a pair of long clippers and gloves and went into the mountains, picking up whatever pine cones you could find that were perfect, very brown and not broken. If there weren't enough on the ground, you had to climb the trees and go out very dangerously to the end of the tallest branches where the cones were. You had to clip off only the cone without damaging the tree. It was very important to me to be careful of the tree so I just clipped the very corners of the ends. Then I would scramble down the tree, twist the cones off the branch, and put them into my gunnysack. I tried to gather at least a gunnysackful a day, about five hundred cones. At three cents apiece that was a lot of money. I could buy a dress or a pair of boots or a hat, something I wanted very much that my parents couldn't afford to buy me.

In the early spring and late summer we would pick gooseberries and currants and sell them to grocery markets. We'd have to go out in knee boots so the snakes couldn't bite us, but we weren't afraid. I wonder if country kids still make their money the way we did. Probably. It was a funny life, being a country kid but going to school in a bigger place. It made me feel I had two different lives and they never quite came together. Life at home was close to nature. It meant doing chores, getting up at six in the morning to milk the cows, chopping wood for the fire, hauling water, feeding the pigs and the baby calves with bottles. Going to school meant being in a place where the girls wore nylons and high heels and mascara. It was hard on us; they used to tease us.

My life has changed so since I got the tape recorder from Dr. Gillman! When Sam is out or Jill is sleeping, I sit down with it and spin out my thoughts. It never talks back. We never have fights. It's a perfect friend. I love it, which may be a crazy thing to say about a machine, but I do. Sam seems jealous of it at times, isn't that funny? I guess before I had the recorder I gave all my attention to him and Jill, and now I have something else. He ought to understand, since music is so important to him, but I'm not sure he does completely.

I feel I really needed the tape recorder. Knowing that I'm off the medication and that I may die sooner than otherwise, it's even more important to me than ever to get these things down in time, before I become too weak or the pain is just too much. So far I'm okay, it's not worse than before. How long that will last I guess no one knows.

Nora is here, helping in the kitchen. I think she's got a thing for Sam. I see her giving him these glances. Does she need him, really? She must have a dozen lovers, all shapes, sizes, and types. Okay, I'm jealous. But she really has been nice, especially about Jill. Nora, please leave my man alone, that's all I ask!

Givits and Weaver are practicing inside. They want to work up their act with Sam so they can get a job at some nightclub. I know their songs inside out by now. Sam is helping clean up after supper. He's good about that. It would be too much for me, with feeding Jill and my leg and all. I'm glad he understands that.

"How're the tapes going?" Nora says.

"It's great," I say. "I love it. It's the most wonderful invention! I almost feel guilty about it."

"Well, anything that makes you so happy can't be bad. Even if it is a machine."

"It's some trip," Sam says, "no two ways about it."

"It's an ego trip, is what it is," Weaver shouts in.

Thanks, pal. Givits says, "What isn't an ego trip? Whatever you dig is an ego trip."

"Even dying," Weaver says.

Nora looks at me. "What's with him?"

In an undertone I say, "He's jealous . . . He thinks I take Sam away from his music. He'd like him to rehearse morning, noon, and night."

"Hey, Sam!" Weaver yells. "Let the chicks clean up, will you? We haven't rehearsed in two weeks."

Nora smiles at me. "I see what you mean." She goes into the next room.

135

I wipe Jill's mouth off. She insists on feeding herself everything, and the result can be kind of a mess.

"Kate," Sam says, sort of low.

I turn around. He's holding the pills Dr. Gillman gave me, the ones she said were a long shot. I haven't taken them for a week. She knows. We talked about it.

"You aren't taking these," Sam says, accusingly.

"They made me sick, just like the others." I hate talking about this with the others right in the next room. "Let's talk about it later."

I turn to go, but he catches my wrist and holds it tight. He's angry. "Let's talk about it *now*."

"I *told* you, they made me sick."

"You didn't give your body time to get used to them. How many did you take? Two? Three?"

"I took them for fifteen lousy days . . . Just stop it!"

"You didn't give the other medication a chance either."

"They made me *sick!* Dammit, is that so hard to understand? These made me dizzy on top of everything else. I fell down. I couldn't take care of Jill. I couldn't think . . . I couldn't even work on my book."

"That damn book is more important to you than living," he says, furious.

"Yes!"

He hurls the bottle of pills into the garbage. "You're out of your head."

"Thanks for being so understanding."

"What about Jill?"

I look at him, feeling torn apart. "It's for Jill I'm doing it!"

"That's some crazy logic."

136

"It isn't!"

"Hey, Sam!" It's Givits from the other room.

Sam gives me one long look full of contempt and goes in to the others.

It's time for Jill's nap. I tuck her in and sneak out, not that they'd notice me anyway, they're so absorbed in their music.

Why can't Sam understand about my going off the medication? It's for him too, that's what's so ironic. He didn't like the person I was becoming either. Making love was lousy, I lay around, hardly able to stir myself. Maybe he thought that was just my being sick, being depressed about it. It wasn't! It was Sam who said I shouldn't think about dying all the time, that I should think about living, about all I wanted to do, about all we wanted to do. That's why I did this, because I knew on the medication I'd never do any of those things. And I'd leave behind nothing, nothing for Jill to remember me. I can't bear that!

About so many other things Sam is understanding. He's not a cruel or a stupid thickheaded person. But I think maybe he's scared. Watching someone die must be different from dying. Not worse, but different. I think it's really he who'd like to pretend that it's not happening, that some miracle cure will come along. Sure, big chance.

I keep thinking of that movie, Love Story, which we saw awhile back. It makes me angry even thinking of it. Her husband was so perfect, so kind, and she always was so lovely—she never even went for medication! Christ! That's so unrealistic! Movies like that should be banned, I think. They make the whole thing so unreal, as though you could die without pain or ugliness. I feel I'm learning something from all this, but at times I'm not sure I want to. I'm not sure I want to see these things in Sam, see his weaknesses. How come *her* hair didn't fall out? Why didn't she throw up every day? How come they never argued about anything because they were both scared and angry at the unfairness of it all! Oh, calm down, Kate. Don't go off ranting. What purpose does that serve? Just get it off my chest, I guess.

When I get back, Sam isn't there. I go downstairs to Nora's apartment to get Jill. "When did they go out?" I ask.

"Oh, around five or so."

"Did they say when they'd be back?"

"Uh uh."

I take Jill up to our place. She seems subdued, quiet. "How is my pooch?" I say, holding her.

"I'm not your pooch . . . I'm your ooch," she says. "You're *my* pooch."

"Where did Daddy go?" I say, as though she would know. But I like talking to her, she's a person, she looks at me with interest, understanding.

"Daddy go?" she repeats. "Men go . . . Catar go."

That's how she pronounces guitar, like it was a sickness. Maybe it is. Maybe it's them who are into an ego trip with all their obsessions about when they'll make it and what they'll do with all that money. Fuck them!

I read some books to Jill. She turns the pages very fast so I just have to make up some kind of commentary on the action as fast as I can. It's funny—she loves the parts where one of the main characters tries to do something

138

antisocial. When the little girl in the story takes out a sharp knife and is reprimanded, Jill's eyes sparkle. "She's bad!" she says excitedly. "She's as bad as Mr. Jones!" Mr. Jones is a tiny peg figure, no bigger than two inches tall with a barely discernible face. Somehow, I forget how, we made up a game where I set him down and say something like, "Now Mr. Jones, you behave yourself. No more wild stuff today. I mean it!" Then I throw Mr. Jones across the room and say, "Mr. Jones, you stop that! What did I tell you?" This goes on with Mr. Jones disobeying all orders to remain in place, and flying all around the room, crashing into things. Jill laughs hysterically; it's her favorite game. Really, she herself isn't so wild. Maybe because she senses she wouldn't be punished, she doesn't have to bother doing anything naughty. I think a lot of my wildness as a kid was a taunting thing, wanting attention, knowing it would get a rise out of someone.

At midnight or so Sam comes in. I've been lying listening to the radio. Some old Bob Dylan songs which I love. "Hi," I say evenly.

He says nothing.

"Thanks for leaving me a note saying where you were going," I say.

"Oh, cut it out!" he says. He pulls off his clothes and gets into bed beside me. "I'm going to call Dr. Gillman tomorrow," he says.

"Why, is your leg bothering you?"

"I don't seem to have any effect on you, whatever I say . . . Well, maybe she will!"

"Sam, I've talked about it with her! She understands why I don't want to continue the medication."

139

"Well, I want to hear it from her own mouth."

"Okay, fine, hear it from her own mouth. But why don't you understand?"

He makes love to me, but he's still in an angry mood. He needs someone and I'm here. God, that's ugly, to think it's become like this when it was so good before. I can feel myself respond physically, but there's nothing joyous in it, no love.

Dr. Gillman is coming for lunch. She's never been here, never seen our place. Even though it's not the most pleasant of occasions to have her, I feel pleased she's coming. I wash and wax the kitchen floor and dust around. I know she's not like my mother. She won't be disapproving if there's a dirty dish in the sink, but I want her to see things looking nice.

Sam goes into the kitchen to make some sandwiches. I sit in the rocker with Jill on my lap.

"How're the tapes coming?" Dr. Gillman asks.

"Wonderful . . . It's the best present anyone ever gave me . . . But let me know, like if you need to make a speech—"

She looks startled.

"You know, you said how sometimes you use it when you have to—"

"Oh, right . . . No, you keep it for now."

"Mustard on your ham?" Sam calls in.

"Thank you, yes," she says.

"If I can get it all down, no, not all of it, maybe that's impossible, but most of what I want to say to Jill, that's all I care about . . . I never could have done it on the drugs. It's weird but I know what it's like to be a drug addict, but in a bad way. I guess I never got any highs from it . . . I know I'll die sooner this way, but—"

"Like tomorrow, maybe?" Sam calls from the kitchen.

"I'm not going to die tomorrow!" I yell back. "Do you want me to?"

No answer.

"No, I figure I'll have a couple of months. And that's all I need."

"Sam, it's Kate's decision," Dr. Gillman says to Sam as he comes in and hands her the sandwich.

"It's *not* Kate's decision!" he says. "Look at her—she's playing Camille! Don't you see? She's on a death trip."

"I'm not . . . I just dig knowing that I'm a person, that I'm capable of love and all it involves. I'm not afraid to love and I'm not afraid to die."

"Bullshit!"

"I think Kate understands that if she goes off all medication she has no chance of prolonging her life. The cancer will grow very fast."

"How fast is very fast?" I say softly.

Sam turns on me. "How can you *ask* that? That's not the issue! With medication you have a chance to live."

"I don't! . . . If I had even a fifty-fifty chance, I would take it. A fifty-fifty chance to live out a normal

142

life . . . I don't, Sam! I have a fifteen percent chance to live five years and on medication those five years will be hell."

"But you'd *be* here. Jill would have you, I'd have you—"

"You wouldn't . . . You'd have a lifeless body, you'd have an ugly, bitchy vegetable . . . I don't want my daughter to remember me that way! I don't want you to!"

"Well, you don't seem all that serene right now."

"I'm not serene because you don't understand. You're fighting me. Dr. Gillman understands and *you* can't!"

Sam looks at both of us. "Look, thirty years ago someone died a day or a week before a cure for diphtheria or pneumonia was discovered . . . Do you want to die a day before they discover a cure for cancer?"

"That's a pipe dream . . . They're not going to discover a cure for cancer in one day."

"Why not? They're working on it . . . Maybe they will."

"I'm afraid I agree with Kate, Sam," Dr. Gillman says. "They are working on it and I feel confident a cure will come. But I'm not sure I'll live to see it, frankly. It's a very complicated thing, cancer."

"But people have breast cancer and live," he says.

"That's different . . . There, surgery and radiation actually can remove it . . . But in bone cancer, that doesn't work . . . Look, I think it could happen many ways. Possibly there'll be an inoculation against cancer like there is for polio and other diseases. There are

143

many ways it can be done. But we're too far from a solution right now."

Sam is silent. Thank you, Dr. Gillman. Oh, I wish I were a billionaire and could leave Dr. Gillman everything. Not that she needs money. I wish I were her fairy godmother then and could give her whatever the one thing is she wants most. "How fast will it spread if she's off the medication?" Sam says, subdued.

"There's no way to predict that . . . It lies in wait, as though it were resting. But when it moves, it moves very rapidly, through the blood."

"But till that happens, till it gets to the lung, I'll have some time, won't I?"

"Some time, yes . . . A few months, possibly."

"And I'm not going to feel much worse than I do now, am I?"

"You'll feel much worse at the very end."

"But up till then—"

"Weaker perhaps, your leg will give you more trouble . . ."

I turn to Sam, though I can hardly bear to. "See? I *do* have time, I have enough time."

"Enough time!" He looks disgusted and angry again. "Enough time for what? To be a wife? To be a mother? To experience everything there is to experience?"

"Sam—" Dr. Gillman says. "It's just not that cut and dried. Kate is going to die. Without medication she will die sooner . . . Some people react so adversely to medication that the difference between dying soon and dying sooner has no meaning to them. Perhaps it's better to die with purpose and dignity, even if it's sooner—"

144

"Okay, maybe it won't do a bit of good to fight it. But if it were me, I would."

"It's *not* you," she says, staring him down.

That gets him. He's suddenly quiet. "Well, if you want my opinion, *you* are committing suicide," he says to me, "and *you*—" he points to Dr. Gillman—"are a murderer." He grabs his jacket and his guitar and slams out the door.

Silence.

"He loves dramatic exits," I say wryly.

Dr. Gillman just stands there. "Kate, try to understand what he's going through."

I shrug. "Thank you, though . . . You were wonderful."

She looks concerned. "Will you manage, Kate, if he doesn't come back?"

"Sure, I'll manage," I say, maybe too quickly.

"You're positive?"

"He'll come back, don't worry . . . He just couldn't stand it that you got the best of him in the argument."

"I wasn't trying to get the best of him."

"I know . . . Maybe that made it worse."

"You're very honest, Kate."

"I guess I don't have time not to be."

She leaves. I give Jill supper and take her to the park, go through the motions. But night comes and morning and night again and no Sam. Maybe she was right. He won't come back. That seems so irresponsible in terms of Jill. Doesn't he care about her, even if he hates me? That really worries me. Who will look after Jill when I die if Sam doesn't? I've thought about this before, but I really have to get it straightened out. I don't like to sit

145

in judgment, but I must make careful choices, for these are the most formative years for Jill.

Sometimes I think Sam and Nora will get together. But Nora doesn't react right to Jill. She's false with her, for one thing, and Jill feels it. I have the feeling that just because Nora had a bad time with her own parents, she would be the same with a child of her own—from lack of knowledge of what a good family life can be. Also, though this is petty as hell too, I don't like the way she keeps house or does dishes. I've always hated a dirty house. It seems to breed discontent and germs. Sam and I always fight when the house becomes a mess.

Nora isn't a good balance for Sam either. He can be difficult and moody at times, and you have to be willing to sacrifice some things for him. And do things for him. I don't think Nora could be that consistent for him. When he yells I have to be calm. When he's outrageous, I have to agree, then tell him he's wrong at a more convenient time. Things aren't easy sometimes.

Jill is a beautiful little girl who needs a mother and a father to love her. Why can't I? I hurt, dammit. I *hurt!* Let me have my child, you bastards of disease! You thieves of lives! May a water buffalo piss on your clean white sheets! So there. Why? Why? Why?

Time time time
See what's become of me
while I sit and think
of my possibilities.

Look around,
grass is high,
it's the springtime

146

of my life—
I'm gonna die.

Sometimes high,
sometimes low,
feelin' mean
and dirty
I see my face
reflected there,
now scarred
what once was pretty.

I'm lonely.

I've been listening to Simon and Garfunkel. God, are they good. I'm going to write all their songs into my book. So that if I have to go into the hospital, I can read them. Some of the verses are so powerful. I really love them.

I am a prisoner upon my throne
of dying midnight roses
forgotten by the many worlds
I once held as my own.
And my frozen words agree
in a whisper I scarcely hear
that the brilliant colors once my own
have faded in the sun.

From my fallen window I see
the now alien ocean
of tides flowing with love
of waves crashing an emotion
I will never experience again
because the happiness
the joys
the soft summer sunlight

148

once my own
have faded in the sun.

As I look across
to the city of confusion
watching
as each moment goes
my tears mark the hours that have passed
and a single winging dove
reminds me of the love
the image of my soul
I once held as my own
and even the sun
is faded.

Nighttime again. Sam's been gone a week. Seven long
days. The days are okay. The house seems quiet without
his music, but I don't altogether mind that. I mind it
some, though. I do miss him. During the day I keep
busy with Jill. We go out a lot, now that it's getting
warmer. She takes her old rag doll and pushes it in the
swing. With other children she mostly sits quietly and
watches them, not quite taking part. Children are
strange, though. The other day one little boy suddenly
said to his sister or friend or whatever, "I hate that girl!"
meaning Jill, who had been sitting quietly to one side.
Doing nothing to bother him at all! Kids maybe aren't
more vicious than adults, but they certainly don't seem
the sweet little creatures they're sometimes painted to
be. I got so furious. I know I should let Jill fight her own
battles. But when that same little boy, later, went over
and out of the blue just started to hit her, I snatched
him up and yelled, "You stop that this second! I mean

it!" I was ready to kill him I was so angry. His mama was this hugely pregnant lady sitting on a bench who sort of waddled over and said lazily, "Peter, you stop that." My heart was beating madly, I was so angry. Then, later, I thought—that was no good. I'm not always going to be around. She has to learn to fight back, to be tough. Jesus. Jill, in any case, was quite impressed by the incident. Several times since then she's said with a big smile, "Mommy hit that boy . . . He was bad!" I don't like to think that kind of physical violence is inherent in men and not in women, but still, Jill does seem to me gentle, trusting, expecting people to treat her well. I can't bear the thought that life will teach her that's wrong!

I let her stay up late on purpose. We watch TV and cuddle up together. Sometimes, she'll lean on my leg and it will hurt. I guess I wince a little because she says, "Mommy's leg hurt?" It comes out "heet" because her r's aren't too good. It seems so sensitive in someone that young, that she senses my pain. Eventually, often when we're watching TV or listening to music, she dozes off and I put her in to sleep.

Then it's night and that's the worst time. I can't keep my mind from circling around dark thoughts, much as I try consciously to push them away. Vague memories invade my mind. I think of the times I've spent and thought, my anger, humiliation, and sometimes despair fight to come again into my mind, to take control and force me through the sorrows I have gained power over. It's so hard to sit and relate these thoughts, even into the tape recorder. My mind continually snaps back to the fears and doubts, the hope that I will live.

150

Then I turn and see Jill sleeping or listen for the phone or a knock at the door. It's easy to be distracted when my mind weighs so heavily with thoughts of leaving it all behind.

I think of that time when we first came to Vancouver, when Jill was just a baby, not yet walking or talking. I remember how my second pill would wear out at about five in the morning and I would lie awake watching the early gray of dawn creep across the smooth white hospital walls, touching first the ceiling, then creeping down against the walls like a fugitive not wanting to be seen. In the middle of a small fold-up bed, Sam lay sleeping fitfully, tossing and turning, trying to keep vigil over me, but too exhausted to keep awake even for a few minutes. The lump on my leg hurt. My mind was full of empty questions it seemed no one could answer. It seemed I had some kind of cancer, but what did that mean? Why? Why? Why? Torments crashing against my brain like a huge boom crushing buildings.

The nurse would come in and take my temperature. "Would you like another sleeping pill, dearie?" she would ask, stroking my forehead. "Can't you sleep?"

"No," I'd say, "but it's soon time to get up anyway."

Sam would stir in his sleep. Soon breakfast would be coming down the long, white corridors; steaming scrambled eggs, oatmeal, juice, four pieces of toast. Sam would eat it all because I couldn't stand to. Somewhere along the line, through all the doctors and hospitals I'd been to, I'd lost all appetite. I knew Sam was hating every bite because I wasn't sharing it with him, but anyway it kept him fed.

After breakfast life came to the hospital once more. If

only for a little while, it at least broke up the monotony of lying in sterile sheets and looking at sterile walls and being afraid to think anything more than sterile thoughts.

Weekends, Sam and I would walk around the sunlit halls, talking, wishing, pouring out our fears to each other. Sam brought me crayons, paper, and a mind puzzle. One day he even brought me a papier-mâché kit to make a statue out of. We filled up all the bedpans we could find with water and proceeded to mix the paste and tear strips of paper to make a statue of one of the nurses, Sue Ellen, but it didn't turn out so well and we had to flush it down my private toilet.

In the chill of the damp night
I run silently, swiftly
to my departure.

I am not yet old enough
for a mind of my own,
for despair and regret.
I am not yet old enough
to be forced down again
into the space
from which I have only just emerged.

As I reach your door, I hesitate.
Will this be the last time?
The last happiness we will know?

What's it like to die? Sometimes, I think I know. It's cold and hard and so lonely. Everybody tries to be nice. I don't know how to react. I wonder what will happen to all my things when I die. Wonder what to do with my books and all the stuff around the house. I hope Sam will remember to water my plants. I'm sort of afraid about dying. I don't regret not taking the drugs. They made me sick in my mind. I didn't care about my family or myself. Or about trying to live, either. I was dead in spirit. I'm just afraid of not knowing what it's like after you die. I don't know how I'll be toward the end. I have to be strong.

In my soul I somehow feel that all is not lost. Maybe I won't die. *Maybe*, though, is a very big word. I sound like a child, I guess. And I'm lonely for the warmth of my mother. "Mama, cradle me again." It is so safe as a child. Mama, I hurt! Kiss it and make it better. Oh I wish!

Who is going to cradle my little Jill? My angel. What's to become of you? Perhaps you'll be okay but I worry so! People, be kind. She's my baby.

There are so many things I wanted to teach her. About life and the way to live and be happy. So much I wanted to talk about. I wanted to help her grow up to be a fine woman, a fine person. I wanted to do what I could to ease the pain of growing up. I don't know what the world will be like for her. Will she be able to breathe clean air or drink pure spring water in the high, free mountains as I did? Will there be war and hatred to fear? Will there even be a world in which she can have a child of her own? If only I knew!

I wish Sam would come back.

The loneliness of the warm spring wind
reminds me you are gone.
A gray shadow on a distant wall

153

marks the time that has passed
since your departure.

The wind has become my constant companion
fashioning lullabys
that whisper your name.
Singing softly of the love we knew,
I think of you,
on still-lingering winter nights.

A month of nights, a year of days,
how long must we wait
for our return
to the place we once knew,
where life was love, and freedom was a song?

How long can we last
in our cells without windows?
We have been forced apart
thru no desire of our own.

Oh wind, whisper to me,
can we return
to life and reality?
Give me a song,
set my heart free.

In the playground I don't talk to many people. I
guess I don't feel like getting close to anyone and then
having to tell them my long, sad story. So I kind of sit
off by myself or bring a book, which I pretend to read.
That was easier in the winter when sometimes Jill and I
were almost the only ones there. Now more people are
coming. Today this very friendly, talkative girl comes

right over and sits down next to me. "Which is yours?" she says.

"The little girl . . . Her name is Jill."

"Oh, she's cute! . . . Mine's the little boy over by the water fountain."

"I don't think it's running."

"Oh, he doesn't care . . . He likes to mess around there." She fishes out a big pile of knitting.

"What are you making?"

"A sweater, I guess. The trouble is, I like knitting, but I hate putting it all together. So I send it to my mother-in-law and she fixes it up."

Jill's nose is running and I get up to wipe it.

"What's wrong with your leg?" the girl says. "By the way, I'm Martha."

"I'm Kate . . . It's . . . I was in a car crash."

"You were? That's really a fantastic coincidence." She yanks up the leg of her blue jeans and points. Her leg is covered with scars which are about half-healed. "That's how I got mine . . . I don't know what I'm going to do when summer comes. I've always looked great in a bathing suit . . . What are *you* going to do?"

"I guess I haven't thought about it too much."

"Was yours your fault? I mean were *you* driving?" Before I can answer she says, "Mine was my fault, that's what's awful about it. I was going too fast and the roads were icy and I skidded and the car burst into flames . . . And *he* was with me." She points to her child.

"Did he get hurt?"

"No, I threw him out of the car . . . It's funny how even in something like that you have presence of mind.

155

Or something. I just threw him out the window and he wasn't hurt at all . . . But my leg was a mess. It's still not so great, but it was awful before. It was just this big mess. I'd just gotten divorced and I was feeling really shitty. I guess it was kind of self-destructive . . . I'm out of all that now. I have boyfriends, I have a job, but then I was really a mess."

I glance at Jill who seems to be playing happily. "Listen . . . do you think you could keep an eye on my little girl for about five minutes? I have to make a phone call."

"Sure, take your time."

There's a phone booth on the corner. I glance back at Jill; she still seems fine. But I just stand in the phone booth a long time. Should I call? It seems so demeaning, somehow. But, then, do I have time for all those games, that whole pride thing?

I know Sam is probably at O'Brien's, this bar where he, Weaver, and Givits have been practicing lately. If he's not, I don't know where he is. I dial the number and it rings seven times. In the middle of the eighth ring Sam's voice says, "Yeah?" He sounds sort of curt, as though he'd been interrupted.

"It's me."

"Hi."

"We've missed you."

There's a moment's pause. "Are you going to take the pills?" he says.

"Jill would love to see you. She—"

"That's not what I asked . . . Just answer the question. You take the pills, I'll come back. It's as easy as that."

"But Dr. Gillman—"

"Fuck Dr. Gillman! I don't want to hear any of that garbage, Kate . . . Will you or won't you, that's all I want to know?"

"You know the answer to that, Sam."

"Well, then you know *my* answer to *your* answer . . . So long."

I stand there, the phone in my hand. The hell with him! And the hell with me for calling. We can manage; Jill and I can do okay. We're not helpless . . . Why are the people I love so wonderfully understanding? With your parents you don't have a choice, but with men you do, unless you're horribly ugly or strange or something. I had a choice. Did I pick wrong two times? But Sam seemed so different from David, so kind. If I had to list half a dozen adjectives to describe Sam, kind would have been one of the first. I remember this poem I wrote about him once:

Soft as a pressed rose's petal
to touch
is your skin.

And dark
as evenings baked in velvet,
your hair.

Fiery,
your breath
as it scorches my back.

And gentle
your hands
as they touch my breast.

157

I love
you,
your kindness,
my lord.

So, I'm a rotten judge of character, I guess . . . I go
back slowly to the playground. Martha is getting ready
to leave. She's nice, but a little nutty. I'm glad she's
leaving because I don't much feel like talking to
anyone. Here I sit, feeling lousy because of Sam and
probably half the women in this park have some such
trouble. Does that make me feel better? No! Next to
me is an elderly lady who beams at Jill. "I bet her
grandma spoils her!" she says, winking at me.

"Her grandmother's never seen her," I say, meanly.
Oh, stop it, Kate! What has that old lady ever done to
you? Is it her fault you pick the wrong men and the
wrong parents?

Sitting here, I let myself feel immersed in self-pity. I
like to sometimes. Like right now because I'm alone.
Because I'm dying. I like being a martyr. At least it gives
me something to be.

I start having a fantasy. It's my old constant worry—
about Jill, what will happen to her. I imagine that in
this park I meet a woman who has one child, but can't
have any more. She's desperate for another child, but
it's so hard to adopt, she doesn't know what to do. I see
her with her own child and she is lovely, a wonderful
mother, kind, gentle, caring. I go over and say: Will you
take my child after I die? She is delighted, can't believe
her good fortune. We smile, Jill seems to like her . . .

Okay, time to go home. End of fantasy.

"Jill, let's go to the plant store, okay, hon?" She trails after me very slowly, pulling a stick behind her.

At the plant store I buy a big pot of ivy. I love having plants around the house. I think it makes the air smell nicer. I lug it home and Jill comes with me while I find a saucer, fill it with water, and put the plant and saucer in the middle of the bay window.

"Ivy grows like mad, Jill, you'll see," I say. "We'll put strings for it to grow on up the sides of the window and across the top. It'll be like a leafy frame. It'll be beautiful."

"I'm wet," Jill says, unimpressed.

"Get me a Pamper, then, okay?"

She trots off and comes back with one. Then she flops down on the bed in the right position. I lean over and kiss her belly button and all around it. "What is this round, fat belly?" I say, nuzzling her. She smiles, indulgently, sleepily. Her lids are heavy; it's past her nap time. By the time I get the Pamper fastened, she's snoring away. I pull the cover over her. The plant does look nice, I'm glad we got it.

In the evening, after supper, Nora drops up. "Is this an okay time?"

"Sure."

"I thought Sam might be practicing or something."

I shake my head. "I mean he may be, but not here . . . He's sort of—cleared out."

She stares at me. "For good?"

"Evidently."

"The bastard! How could he? How rotten! . . . Jesus, I thought you two seemed so happy. You're the only happy couple I've ever seen."

I shrug.

"How do you like that? Wow, men are something, aren't they!"

I like talking to other women, but I've never liked

that kind of general "aren't men awful" type of conversation. It seems so general; it never helps.

Nora flops onto the bed. She's wearing some crazy getup, looks a little like Jill when she's doing her gypsy mama bit. "Well, I had a fight with my guy yesterday, but we never—it wasn't like you and Sam."

"Which guy was that?"

"Willie, the black guy . . . You saw him that time, didn't you?"

"Oh yeah, I think so."

"Look, nobody's happy," she says, "so why should we be? Why should we be exceptions? My parents hated each other's guts for forty years."

"Mine didn't," I say.

She looks surprised. "Didn't they?"

"No, they loved each other . . . They still do, I think."

"I thought you said your mother was a bitch."

"Well, we don't get along, but . . ."

"Well, my mother no one could have liked, much less loved . . . She was crazy, God rest her whatever. I mean, you know, not like a little off, but the kind that should have been locked up in a padded cell."

In some ways I envy Nora her unequivocal hatred of her mother. If I didn't love Mom it would be a thousand times easier.

"Nora." I look away. "Nora, I'm kind of tired . . . Jill and I were out all day . . . would you mind if I—"

"Oh, go on, go to sleep . . . I have some stuff to do. I just wanted to say hi, see how things were."

After she leaves, I just lie there. The nighttime blues

161

are settling over me. I wish I had a piano. I could play lullabies for Jill. Nora's nice, people have been nice, but there isn't anybody I can cry with. Nobody to touch me. Nobody to say it's okay. Nobody to comfort me and listen to my self-pity. I'm so tied up inside it hurts . . . I wish Pat could come up again.

Maybe I'll call home. If Pat's there, I'll ask her to come up. I have enough money for her ticket.

"Hi, Mom, I hope it isn't too late to call."

"Well, your father is in bed . . . I was just doing some things . . ."

"How are you?"

"Oh, as well as can be expected, I guess . . . How are you?"

"We're all fine too . . . Is Pat there?"

"What do you want to say to her?"

"I just felt like talking to her."

"She's out."

"Oh . . . Well, actually I called because I was wondering if she might . . . come up again."

"We don't have the money for that, Kate."

"I can pay for it, Mom . . ."

"Pat's too young to travel alone."

"She came before."

"I know."

"Why don't you come too? It's not that expensive if you come by bus. Jill is so great now. She talks so well . . . I should think, being her grandmother, you'd want to see how she was coming along and all . . ."

"Kate, have you called up just to criticize me for my behavior?"

"No."

162

"How is Sam?"

"Okay, he's not here right this second."

"Oh?"

"He's . . . rehearsing."

"Where?"

"I don't know . . . He moved out."

"Are you getting another divorce, then?"

"No, it's not . . . He just—it's hard for him with my knee . . . and he doesn't have a job yet."

"You mean he still doesn't have a job! I can't *believe* that!"

"Mom, stop it, will you!"

"That to me is simply scandalous."

"Okay . . . Listen, if Pat comes in later, tell her what I said, okay? That she should come up."

"I don't know, Kate . . . Pat is so young. I don't want her getting into all kinds of trouble."

"What kind of trouble is she going to get into playing with Jill and helping me clean up the apartment?"

"You know what I mean."

"I *don't* know what you mean."

"I should think now that you're a mother, you would understand. Mothers worry—"

"Okay, okay . . . Forget it, then. It was great talking to you, Mom. I'd forgotten what a sweetheart you are. So long."

I'm shivering. I'm turning to ice. Ugh. Why did I do that? Why did I call? Why in the name of anything did I tell her Sam had left? It's weird how you do certain things again and again, get the same reaction and yet go on expecting a different one. She doesn't have to know Sam has left. So why did I tell her? To make her feel

163

sorry for me maybe, all alone? To make her send Pat? . . . But that never works with her. She hates people who beg for things from her. She thinks pride is the most important virtue in the world . . . Why did I tell her Sam doesn't have a job? I guess, indefensible as it is, I want to be honest with her. If I lied and pretended things that weren't so, it would seem to be proving all she said of me was true. It isn't that I knew Pat would come and see Sam wasn't here and go back and tell her. I just want there to be truth and openness between us. Bullshit, as Sam would say. You have to build openness on something and we don't have that something.

I fall asleep late, really late. For a while I lie awake listening to the tapes I've done. It's funny hearing your own voice. I don't quite sound like me. But that must be how I sound to others . . . I don't listen long. Talking to Mom got me too down, way down. I want to sleep.

All of a sudden, I hear footsteps. My heart starts pounding. Don't let it be a burglar. We have nothing to rob. I call out loudly, "Who is it?" hoping that if they know someone's home, they'll go away.

"Bob Dylan," a voice says. It's Sam!

He comes into the room, guitar on his back, carrying a funny-looking tiger cat. Seeing the tape recorder, he grins. "Making love to your machine?"

"It's a nice alternative," I say, staring him down. "It doesn't walk out when things get sticky. It doesn't argue. It's not stupid. Or bullheaded—"

"Well, I hope the two of you have a wonderful life together." He hands me the cat. "This character was

164

hanging around O'Brien's . . . I thought you might like him." He walks past me into the bedroom.

I begin stroking the cat. What a funny creature, one ear looks like it's mashed down on one side. "Did you come back for your stuff?"

"Yeah."

"Odd time to move, isn't it?"

"Jill's asleep."

"So it's easier?"

"Much easier."

I watch him as he begins taking things out of the drawer and throwing them in his bag. "Want me to shut up too? Or doesn't it matter one way or the other?"

"I'm immune to you."

I just stand there, watching him. It's as though he was at the wrong end of a telescope, a million miles away, very small. A strange feeling. "What's the cat's name?"

"Gypsy."

"Is that symbolic or something?"

"Descriptive."

"I like him . . . He seems to like me."

"He's dumb. He might."

I can't help smiling, he's trying so hard not to say one nice thing. "I miss you and your snotty remarks."

Sam turns. After a second he says, "I miss you too . . . You and your death wish."

"That's gone."

"Sure."

"I mean it."

He looks puzzled. "You're going to take the drugs?"

I shake my head. Then suddenly I find myself saying,

"Let's go to the mountains, Sam, away from all this, you and me and Jill. It would be so good . . ."

"It would be the same."

"It wouldn't have to be."

"What about the cancer? What're you going to do about it?"

"Live with it."

"You're asking me to watch you die, baby . . . I can't."

"I'm not . . . Don't watch me die . . . Just stay for now . . . Please, Sam. I beg you . . . If you can't take it at the end, then go."

Slowly, he puts down his guitar and comes over to me.

I'm not going to cry. I just stand there and let him hold me. "People do things different ways," I say, very low. "Just respect my way, that's all. Understand it."

He strokes my hair. "I missed you a lot . . . I wanted you a lot."

"I wanted you . . . It's been lousy. I called Mom tonight."

He laughs. "You must have been desperate!"

"I wanted Pat to come. She said no."

"That figures."

"How's it going, with your rehearsing and all?"

We lie on the bed together. "It's good." But he isn't paying attention. He's moving toward me, on top of me, his lips on mine.

Okay, so I had no pride, Mom, and it worked. So you're wrong, see? Sometimes it works. I don't have time for pride.

166

Autumn is the time for loneliness
and love
that died in the forgotten sun.

The time for being alone
in your world,
to decide answers for all the questions
that summer brought.

The time to write unfinished poems
and sing unfinished songs
before winter freezes them forever.

The time to end,
and begin again
as we always do,
anyway . . .

167

Finally. Peace, within myself. Summer is over and fall is my time, my poetry. I love it. September and changing leaves, falling, cluttering, drifting to the ground. The smell of the sun, the dying grass, the light filtering through the branches. In autumn the sun is in the peace position. It's time for warm sweaters and football and touching and loving. Oh, I love it all so much.

It's been good since Sam came back. Of course, he's not always around, but I wouldn't want that. He has to have his music. I would never ask him to give that up just to be with me. Anyway, I have my tapes and that makes a lot of difference. Sometimes, I think I'm trying too hard to say something meaningful in them. Sometimes, my mind just goes blank. I don't feel at ease. It's hard to put it down when I'm worried Sam will hear it all eventually. It's not that I have anything to say that he shouldn't read, but it's hard to write about things that hurt and things that need to be thought out privately when you know someone else will be reading them.

Still, I feel like I've come to terms with things more, whether because of the tapes or Sam being understanding or what. Cancer is really a very bad disease, that's true, but I think there're other things I wouldn't want to have either. I don't think I would want to have multiple sclerosis or, I don't know, something that would make me lose my mind somehow but still let me retain my body. I wouldn't want to be mentally retarded. I wouldn't want to have to be normal in every respect and yet not able to communicate with people. I didn't think it would be as easy to cope with just having cancer. I mean, cancer hurts. You get it and it grows and it grows and you know that your chances are very slim. It seems, though, like there are other things that are at least as bad. What I'm trying to say is that I'm not that badly off, even though I'm dying. There're worse ways to go, I guess. I don't know, maybe I won't feel that way at the end if it hurts much worse and I can't breathe. Even now I get tired fast, I can't do so much around the house. So I don't know how I'll feel later when it gets worse than this. Maybe I won't feel that way at all.

The dilemmas of dying are many. You can't figure out if you want to be buried or cremated, embalmed or not, what clothes you want to be buried in, what you want on your gravestone. What is natural? That's what I have to decide. Or at least what would feel most natural to me. What would give me the best chance of getting back to this earth if reincarnation does happen? I mean, you read ashes to ashes, dust to dust . . . What does that mean?

I guess I like the idea of cremation for the thought of having my ashes spread across the mountains. I see Sam, standing tall, the wind whipping his long hair, with a beautiful vase in his hand, tossing my ashes out into the wind, quickly dissipating into nothingness, gone as quickly as I came into the world so many years ago.

That's so romantic, though, and that is the only part of cremation I can think of that I like. I envision myself being burned, the flesh snapping and crackling in the fire, my flesh falling away from the bone. No, maybe I don't want to be cremated.

So that leaves being buried. I hate the thought of being stuffed inside a box and put into the ground. I dig

169

the idea of having a gravestone to write something on, though. I like the idea of having some music played for me and would like the idea of flowers if they weren't from the florist, I mean, so deathly looking. They should be beautiful, free-form field flowers—Queen Anne's lace, roses, daisies, to signify not just death, but a passing on, a freedom that I will have achieved.

I want just to be buried in a pair of shorts or one of the skirts Sam bought me, and a comfortable shirt, not something stiff and unnatural. I want just a simple wood coffin, with old-fashioned handles and a soft plush inside and a nice pillow. I don't want a metal casket, that isn't natural. How can you return to the earth in a metal that won't rot?

The music I want is John Denver's *Country Roads*.

Today I tried to write a poem for Jill, but all I could think of—the only words beautiful enough—were:

Beautiful Sunshine

That's what she is to me and no other words express it. So, no poem, Jill—but much love, much care, much giving to you.

When we're up in the mountains, it's almost as if I can forget everything bad, the bitter thoughts, and think only constructively. Then we come back and real life is there; going to the hospital, all of that.

This time when we pull up in front of our apartment, Weaver is sitting on our steps. "Where've you been?" he says to Sam. "We had an audition. We had a job. Nearly. Except you weren't there."

I glance at Sam. I didn't know he had an audition. If I'd known, I'd never have suggested we get away this

170

weekend. It was my birthday, that was why I wanted to go this particular weekend—I'm twenty now, not a teen-ager anymore. A grown-up lady, a woman. Still, even my birthday could've waited, if what Weaver says is true. You never can tell with him.

We all go inside and Sam brings the groceries we bought into the kitchen. "We had to go to the mountains," he says.

"Without telling anybody?" Weaver says. "I mean, you knew about the audition, man . . . What're you doing?"

"Lay off," Sam says.

I guess he doesn't want to say it was my birthday. Not that Weaver would consider that a very good excuse. I go in to get a fresh Pamper for Jill. As I'm passing Weaver, he says, "How's the big C, Kate?"

He hates me so much! Wow, I suppose I should feel honored. But it just makes me feel rotten. I knew coming home would be a matter of coming down to earth, but I thought it would be drifting down gradually, not falling with a thud on pointed rocks. I don't even answer, just go to Jill.

Sam says angrily, "I said, lay off."

"I was feeling a lot better before you showed up, thanks," I can't help putting in.

"Oh, right," Weaver says. "Now you're going to have to rush right back up to the mountains, aren't you, to recuperate from nasty old Weaver . . . Your old man doesn't need to work."

"Weaver," Sam says.

But he goes on in that same sarcastic voice. "Nothing is more important than dying. You don't need money, you're 'above' money. You don't have hospital bills. Rent. Gas. You don't buy shoes. Jill never needs shoes . . . It's really a great life. As long as you've got parents you can soak."

Sam grabs him. For a second I think he's going to sock him one and almost wish he would. But he just turns away. He looks depressed.

Weaver goes on, "The guys they got, it's pathetic. Keith Wilder and Gordon Matthews. Sam, you *know* we're better than they are. You know we would've gotten the job if only we'd been there. If only she—"

"It's my fault," Sam says. "Leave Kate out of this."

I look at him, but he's looking at Weaver who's settled into a chair. Weasel would be a better name for him with those little eyes and scruffy hair. "I'm splitting," he says.

"Good," I say.

"The group?" Sam is shaken, I can tell.

"I've got to make money."

"Sam'll do better as a single," I say.

"He won't do anything as a single."

"Sam, are you hungry? Do you want a beer?"

"Sure, thanks."

"I'll have one too," Weaver says.

I get two beers and hand one to each of them. "What do you need money for?" I say. "You eat all our food. You drink all our beer."

"Well, you've wrecked my life," he says. "I might as well be into you for something."

"Oh come on. Wrecked your life! How?"

"I came all the way up here, knowing Sam and I

172

could form a good group . . . I could've stayed in Denver and—"

"Oh bull! You did what you wanted, Weaver! Don't dump it on us!"

"Why do you think I won't make it as a single?" Sam says carefully.

How can Sam take him seriously? I get so angry at that. "He's jealous, that's why. He knows he won't make it as a single because he's such a nurd and he's scared you will."

"I love you too, baby." He looks at Sam. "Okay, I'll tell you why, since we're having a big truth session here . . . You don't work anymore, even *when* you work, if you follow me. Your head's not there . . . And—you just don't work enough. Christ, remember when we were starting, we used to work every night, night after night . . . Music doesn't mean enough to you anymore."

There's a long silence.

"That's a dumb lie," I say.

"No, it's the truth," Sam says quietly. "What'll you do, on your own?" he says to Weaver, not angry.

"I used to sell stuff," Weaver says. "Before I ran into you and Givits." He looks over at me. "Hey, Kate, you're at the hospital a lot. You've got access. How about it? . . . Seems like you kind of owe it to me, kid."

I look at Sam, startled.

"That's not very funny," he says.

"It wasn't meant to be."

"Then get out."

"Who? Me—or her?"

173

"Get out before I kill you."

"Oh, wow . . ." He raises his beer can. "I want to drink to this early John Wayne on my left."

Sam gets up and grabs the can out of Weaver's hand and hurls it across the room. It hits the wall and beer dribbles down on the floor. Weaver gets up. In a mocking voice he says, "And don't come back till you've apologized to my wife."

"Right."

"Forget it, pal, forget it." He walks out, slamming the door.

I stare after him. "Thank God . . . I wish he'd left months ago . . . I wish he'd never come here after you."

"He's a damn fine musician," Sam says slowly.

"So what! I don't care *what* he is! He's a rotten, mean person."

Sam rubs my shoulders. "I'm sorry, Kate."

"If he's such a damn fine musician, why's he so scared stiff about making it without you?"

"Well, together, we were good . . . Look, I think he's right, frankly. I'll never make it by myself, either."

"So, you'll form some other group."

"Sure, only—"

"Anyway, how do you know? Maybe you *could* make it alone. Just because *he* says—"

"No, I couldn't, Kate . . . I don't mean I'm not good. I'm not knocking myself . . . Look, we had something good, the three of us. He was right. We would've gotten the job. I just feel it."

"Then blame him . . . for walking out now. Don't blame me!"

After a second he says, "I'm not blaming you."

174

"It was my birthday. That's why we went . . . Why didn't you tell him that?"

He shrugs.

"We didn't even have to go . . . Why didn't you tell me you had the audition? I would've understood."

He just looks pained. "I guess I should've. I just thought—"

"What?"

"I don't know."

"Sam, listen, we've got to be honest with each other. Without that, it's just stupid, it doesn't make any sense."

"Yeah, you're right." He sits down. "I don't know . . ."

"What?"

"I just think maybe he's right . . . My heart isn't in it anymore. You have to give all of yourself to it."

"Well, then give it, if that's what you want! Don't sit around waiting for me to die so you can do that! That's sick! How does that make me feel?"

"I can't, Kate . . . I don't have it in me."

"Okay, then accept that."

"I try to . . . Then I think, if only this hadn't happened."

"My getting sick?"

He nods, not looking at me.

"I know!"

"I guess I don't believe in God especially," he says, "but if he does exist, he ought to be drawn and quartered . . . He must be some sick-joke artist."

"Maybe he's like Weaver," I say, smiling. "I mean, he just happened to have this knack for stuff like creating

175

the world and man and all . . . But he's a moral idiot, he has a pea for a brain when it comes to anything else."

Sam smiles. We sit side by side. I rub his hand. "You're good," I say.

"Am I?"

"Yes." I can't say anything more, though I'd like to.

"Where's Jill?"

"Inside . . . sleeping."

He glances up. "How long do you think she'll—" He draws me down on the bed.

"Long enough."

The sun is streaming in the window. Beautiful sunshine.

How's this for anticlimaxes? Weaver and Sam are back together again. It was Givits who "reconciled" them, which I think was sweet in a way. He said they had so much going together, it was a shame to break it up now, that they should just put personal differences to one side. There's kind of a prickly, competitive thing between Weaver and Sam, whereas Givits always seems older. They both listen to him. I'm not sure he really is that much older—it's his manner. Anyway, be that as it may, they're off rehearsing again, auditioning.

I'm glad. I don't want the guilt of feeling Sam wrecked his career for my sake. Like all those crummy movies on the late late show. He ruined his career for a mere woman. Not that the mere woman part appeals to me, but music and Sam are too much one to be parted.

And maybe he's right. He may be good, but not in a way that would show to best advantage in solo.

It makes me laugh, though. After that big "scene." I guess life is like that. Pulling these little surprises.

Today Sam is off rehearsing and I'm lying here, daydreaming. I like to sometimes, to go into the past. Guess there's not too much future to think about. I remember that first day Sam and I spent together, not the day we met, but the one after, after I'd spent the night at his place. We had coffee and toast and kept staring at each other. Doing all those things together, brushing our teeth etc. seemed so natural. He had this big black hat on, probably stolen from some theater set, which really made him look dramatic. He showed me some pictures he'd painted, watercolor sketches. I liked them. I liked his apartment which was small, but looked comfortable, lived-in. It gave me a feeling of being home. He played the guitar for me like a madman, shouting with joy the few songs he knew, sometimes drawing his brows together as if that would make him sound better. Then gently, he would stroke the strings to make the music he had written in his head, bending over the guitar like it was a precious gift. He played with such compassion and finesse. He's a great guitarist because he loves what he does and plays from his heart. Sometimes, he plays when he's sad and it's so beautiful I want to cry, but don't, because he's so sensitive and tender that he would never play again that way if I did.

I like his eyes. They can look so fierce and wicked with passionate hate for what he dislikes and sometimes so round and innocent and so deep I can see far into them. They hold a lot of love for almost everything he

178

touches. I like what we have between us now. It's been scratchy lately, but it's growing back. We love together, just him and me and our little Jill and no one gets in unless we want them. We need only each other. I love Sam because he's warm and compassionate, because he says to me, "Kate, I love you," and I know he means it. I don't ever want to leave him. I love him. Now I'm thinking how unfair it is. A tear wells up and creeps down my cheek. Love is not something you can live or die without.

I wonder why I haven't heard from the hospital. Last week they took a new series of tests to see how things were going. I would've expected they would call to tell me the results. I'm worried. I'm afraid I know already. I guess it makes no difference.

I had some pretty strong thoughts on dying last night. When I'm lying in bed, it's hard not to think about it. It's so damned unfair. To me, to Jill, to Sam. I just can't understand it at all. I can't understand the way all of this works into the scheme of things. Why doesn't it at least have some purpose! It has only brought me pain and my family pain. Why?

Sam is right, though. I've still got a lot of living to do before it's time to die. Guess I should do some. My time is running short. I should make a list of all the things I want to do before I die. There are so many things!

I want to finish my book for Jill. I want a piano. I want to learn to play beautiful songs. I always have wanted to, but somehow never got around to it. I want to finish the quilt I started and some tea towels and pillowcases and sheets to put in a cedar chest for Jill and

I want to put some other things in too. I don't know what exactly. Just little things she'll need someday. Mostly a lot of love.

I want to make things good between Sam and me. I know the best thing I could do would be to make love the way we used to, but I just can't, it hurts so. I want to give him so much, whatever there is I can do to prove my love and devotion. I wish I could give him of all things a motorcycle. But more than commercial things, material things, I want to give him all of myself. If I'm any good at all, then he truly deserves me, for he deserves any and all things that are good.

There are lots of little things I want to do. Fill this book, knit Sam a sweater, grow my hair long. I pray for time.

Going to the hospital. That familiar building. I don't dread it anymore. They've been good to me and that means a lot. At first, when I went to Riverdale and found out that I had cancer, I felt only fear and anger and worst of all hate toward the medical profession for not having something to help me with. But after coming to Niles, I feel so very different. I've learned so much that I'm actually, in ways, thankful for the opportunities I've had, from being sick. They've all been so kind and thoughtful that I can't help but think of the hospital as an island in my high sea of trouble. When I come there, I feel very safe and cared for and that's quite a change from the fear I used to know.

I'm so glad they understood, finally, about my going off the drugs. I think they saw that for some people it really is better to die in peace of mind than in the

181

turmoil that I felt about the situation. If a person can accept the drugs and the pain of it all, then I say, right on, give the best you've got. But to those who can't, I'm glad they had the insight to let it be. I love them, and especially Dr. Gillman, a lot for that. It really has, I feel, given me a lot of inner strength.

"Sam will meet me here later," I tell Dr. Gillman. "He said the audition would be over at nine-forty, but—"

She's looking at me in a funny way. "Has he got the adoption papers for Jill yet?"

"No, he hasn't even applied . . . Why?"

"Here it is, Kate."

Somehow, I knew today would be the day. I knew it when I woke up, but still, at her words, something freezes inside me and my mouth gets dry. We look at the X ray together. The spot is there. It's in the lung.

"How much time does that leave me?"

"Not much."

"Weeks? Months? Days?"

"It's hard to say."

When Sam comes to pick me up, he looks so elated, I don't say anything. He's sure they did well this time, that they may have a job. "Keep your fingers crossed, baby."

"I will."

I feel bad that just as things are working out for him, I'm going. Not just for me, but I wish I could be more a part of his happiness.

When we come home, he tucks me into bed and turns on the TV, then goes out. Where? To Nora? I have the feeling he's slept with her, maybe in that time we were apart. Just from little things he's let drop. No, I haven't found lipsticked handkerchiefs in his pocket. Well, she knew things were bad with us, I told her . . . and he needs someone, someone alive, living. I understand it. Still, I have moments of feeling bitter like now when he just vanishes and leaves me here alone. I think I've become repulsive sitting in bed. I'm getting upset by the whole situation. If I am repulsive, if I am upsetting to be with, boring to be with, then please, God, do something so that our relationship isn't wrecked, so that there's something good to remember at the end. For surely neither of us needs the pain that not getting along brings us.

Sam doesn't realize what it's like, I don't think. When I get to feeling down, he thinks I'm just feeling sorry for myself. I know I do, but is that so wrong? I'm losing an awful lot and it's not really easy. But he could help by being kinder sometimes. I don't know. Maybe it's just me. Lately he seems different, maybe because his music is going better and he's so involved in that again. It seems like he's always acting up in front of friends, trying to make them notice him, doing things he would never have done before. He doesn't care about his appearance anymore. I used to love it so much when he dressed nice. And he did too, but now, sometimes I'm ashamed of how he looks. Maybe that's petty, but it's important to me that he looks nice. It shows that he cares. Maybe he just doesn't care anymore. I wish he'd wait to be a slob till I die. I love him for the way he is inside. Not all the stuff he's been doing to impress people. It confuses me. I don't know. I guess I love him despite myself.

Jill has been gone this weekend visiting Sam's parents. I miss the little stinker so much. She's been my rod, my staff, through my whole sickness. She's been my comfort and I desperately need her. I shouldn't have sent her away. Still, it's been good for Sam. I guess I'm bitter. I get bitter when I can't go to the bathroom and Sam has to bring me the bedpan. Or when my leg drips gory, ugly juices. I feel so repulsive. I feel bitter when I look at pictures of Jill and realize that soon I won't even be able to see pictures of her. I won't get to touch her or be with her or remember her. Oh, how I wish that at least in death you could remember. I wonder if you can. I doubt it, death being not proud. What does that mean, I wonder. It means to me that death isn't afraid to come and take you away, no matter who you are, which is upsetting. I have so much to give, so many things to do, so many people to be—and I'm not going to get to do it.

Sam has a job! He came back late last night so excited. I am too. It's at O'Brien's, that place they used to hang out. They have a great audience, he said, people that know music, people that buy records. Maybe in six months they'll have an album out. He was so pleased, so happy, that I got carried along and that was good. Since I'd heard that news at the hospital, I'd been really low. Now my mood seems to have lifted. Jill is back, talking away, chattering about everything, seeming so happy. Just seeing the two of them like that, into their own things, makes me feel good. The job is two nights a week. I'm so proud of Sam. He's wanted this for so long.

When something good like this happens, you kind of regret a lot of other things. I regret that ugly scene with

185

Weaver that time. Even though I think he was mean. Now, since they got the job, he's actually been nice to me. Trying to be, anyway.

Givits may get married. He was here with his girl, her name is Maria. I liked her. She thinks he's the greatest thing that ever lived.

"He married us," I say. I'm tucked up in my blanket, feeling warm and snug. I like to remember that day.

"How was it?" she asks. "Was he good?"

"It was wonderful . . . sort of crazy, though. It was in the hospital."

"Oh?" She looks uneasy. Does she know about me? Maybe just that I'm sick.

"We'd just come here, we weren't even planning on it, we just thought we'd live together like we had been, but then—my divorce papers came through and—"

Givits and Sam are talking about something with their music.

"Your little girl is so sweet," Maria says. "She gave me this." She shows me a small doll.

"Yeah, she likes to do that, to give people presents."

"Aren't you excited—about their opening night?"

"Oh sure . . . It'll be great . . . I probably won't go, though. Im not sure I—"

"Of course you'll go!" Sam says loudly. "What do you mean?"

I don't feel like talking about it in front of them so I just say, "I guess I will, then."

When they go, Sam goes in to give Jill her bath. I'm just not up to that anymore. It tires me too much. Anyhow, I think she really digs having him fix it for her, towel her off. I don't blame her. I used to be like that with my dad.

I tried writing my parents a letter a few nights ago, but I don't know. Is it worth it? I guess I wanted to try to say all I felt, especially about how it's been bad these last few years. But it didn't come out right. More a kind of pleading that I didn't want. But suddenly the phone rings and it's Mom. I can tell from her voice she feels she had to call. There's that "duty" sound, not especially a loving sound.

"I gather Sam is back?" she says. "You said—"

"Yeah, he . . . He's even got a job!"

"What type of job does he have?"

"Playing the guitar . . . That's what he does, you know." Oh, don't let me get mad at her. Why does she have to sound that way, like an FBI agent?

"Does he get paid?"

"Of course he gets paid, Mom . . . He belongs to the union. They have to pay him . . . It's a regular job."

In the background I can hear Jill splashing around and Sam playing with her.

"How much does he get paid?"

"A lot! . . . Mom, listen—"

Luckily, just as I'm about to blow my cool, once and for all, Sam comes in and takes the phone from me. "Hi, Mother? This is King Kong and I'll tell you how much I get paid. I get paid four thousand dollars a week, and we're going to buy this fantastic mansion with six swimming pools and a gold bathroom and maybe, maybe if you're real good, you can come visit us. Okay?" And he hangs up.

I'm laughing, out of nervousness mainly, but I can't stop. I double over, clutching my sides.

"Your mother is a real mother, you know that?" he says, going back to Jill.

"You shouldn't have, Sam."

"Shouldn't have! . . . I should've said a lot more that I'm just too polite and well-bred to say to a lady."

"Why is she like that, though?"

"Honey, you know the answer to that."

"But, like, her life was hard, but was it so much harder than anyone else's?" I begin thinking of Sam's mother of whom I've certainly voiced various ill-humored comments in my time. Only—she loves Sam. I mean, say whatever you like about her, she's narrow-minded or petty or has the wrong values, but she loves him, right down to her toes, even when she can't understand why he does what he does—and she rarely can. Still, there's always that rock-bottom thing which is there, no matter what.

Jill comes shrieking out of the tub. "Put your night-gown on, baby!" Sam says, running after her.

"I don't want to!" Jill says, leaping up on the bed with me. "I want to tuck in with Mommy."

"Hon, you'll be cold with nothing on." But she is already deep down under the covers, the sheet pulled up to her chin, looking at us with mischievous eyes. I peek under the sheet. "I see a belly button down there."

She squirms up and pulls up my shirt. "I see Mommy's belly button." She pushes against my breasts, what there is of them now that I'm so thin. Playfully she squeezes them. "Someday Jill will have breasts too," I say.

She looks thoughtful, considering this. "I don't want them . . . They flop!"

"Not necessarily."

"I'm not going to have them," she declares.

"Okay, hon."

"Hey, ladies," Sam calls from the kitchen. "Are you two going to rise for supper . . . Or shall I serve you in bed?"

"In bed!" Jill yells, excited.

"No, we'll get up," I say. I hate being that much of an invalid. I can still make it to the table, at least.

"Shall I heat up this chicken?"

"Sure." I hate it that Sam has to do everything now, all the cooking, tidying up. He's good about it, he doesn't complain, but I don't like it. That's old-fashioned, I guess. But I did like cooking and keeping the house nice. I miss doing those things.

Boy, Sam's mother doesn't let anything go by, does she? She had to go and get Mr. George to get the adoption papers for Jill. Christ, I hate to think what Sam would do without her. Jesus, if she doesn't lay off, Sam is never going to do anything for himself. I realize she is maybe trying to be helpful, but she is just one big nuisance. She's so sure she's going to get Jill. I'll bet—well. I won't say, but I bet my wishes won't be carried out when I die. She finally told Sam's father about everything and tried to blame the fact that we hadn't told him before on me. I remember asking both her and Sam to tell him—but no, it had to be their way. I don't know what they planned to do when Jill got old enough to know the truth.

Sam can sense I'm irritated about it. "Look, hon, I

190

just haven't had time. With our show opening in a day or so."

"I know!"

"I'll take care of Jill. The papers are in my name."

"You'll be too busy. With your work and all—"

"I'll find a way."

I want to believe him so much I let myself believe him. What happens will happen. What I say doesn't matter much, I guess. And really, if Jill is happy that is the main thing. Ideally, I would like her raised by someone who felt as I do about life. I'm sure there are such people in the world, I'm not a freak. The next best thing is that she be raised in a way that brings her happiness. After all, I don't exactly approve of how my parents raised me, but I still had a lot of happiness as a child and have certainly had a lot as an adult. It's just stupid to aggravate myself with torments over Jill's future. Children are strong. And somehow I feel she will remember me, even if not in any conscious way. What we've had together will be there and she can come back to it.

This dying thing is getting to be such a drag. I've been sitting in bed all day long because my chest hurts too much to move. Just now I got up to go to the bathroom for the first time and my leg started bleeding extremely hard and fast. It scared me so much. I don't know what to do, it's all so scary.

The raindrops are falling down my window like molten jewels. The car lights flicker and sparkle as the tires write melodies splashing the water against the curbs.

My chest is hurting so very badly. I spend my days

191

now sitting up in Sam's lounge chair or in bed, propped by pillows, trying hard, struggling sometimes, to breathe. The TV is my constant companion. I watch all the repeats, the specials, the soap operas, laughing at the last, because my life would fit so well in that market.

I haven't written any poems lately, haven't felt like it. I've had so many thoughts to categorize, so many fears and ideas, so angry with myself for being sick. Here's one from a few weeks ago that I worked over a little:

I can't see you
in another's arms—
smoothing back the wrinkles
on your forehead.

I can't help but cry
to think of another
telling you it's okay
when you've had a lonely day.

Seems like only yesterday
I began to share your bed,
and like the gentle rain,
you've let me share your head.

I hate to see it end
and yet, baby,
maybe things will be better
when the days are shorter
with the winter of my life—
and finally freedom in the spring.

I've been thinking lately
of my life.
It's been a good one,

nice just to hang around.
How long it's been since this mornin',
seems like it was only yesterday, my baby.

I play with Gypsy, my cat. Ah, she's so wicked. Grabbing me with feet and mouth, so feisty. Never does she use her claws or teeth, she's so loyal. She sleeps with me at night, lies with me all day, leaving only to eat or go outside for a while. I think she thinks I'm her mother.

Sam comes in, gives me a kiss. Kind of a perfunctory one, but maybe I'm getting hypersensitive. "That's not the usual kiss," I say, half to myself.

He grins. "I'm higher than a kite, that's all . . . In exactly six hours we hit the big time."

"I know . . . I wish I could be there."

"You're going to be there."

"Jill's just got over her cold. I don't—"

"You're going to leave her . . . Nora said she'll take her . . . I want you with me."

I look at him, puzzled. There's something a little funny, not quite direct here. Should I push it? "What's going on, Sam?"

He looks pained, trapped. "I just want you there. What's wrong with that?"

I can't answer. I don't know the answer.

"Kate? What's wrong with that? Tell me."

Finally, I look right at him. I can't bear this game-playing between us. It makes me sad. "Are you having an affair?"

"You can't stand anybody else in center stage, can you?"

193

"That wasn't the question."

"Daddy!" Jill calls from the kitchen.

"The answer obviously is no," Sam says, still uncomfortable, not quite looking at me. "Absolutely and categorically no."

"Say that without squirming."

"Daddy!"

He goes in to Jill, glad to escape. I didn't want to make you feel guilty, Sam. It doesn't matter. Is there a way to say it that sounds believable, not phony? I call after him, "Sam . . . it's okay."

I sigh. If I'm going tonight, I'd better take a pain pill just before I set out. Sitting that long, all that noise—I better not pass out, that would be great. I do want to go, but in some ways I feel it might spoil it for Sam, seeing me looking so awful and gaunt.

We leave Jill with Nora. Jill is sleepy and goes without a protest. I'm glad. I don't have the strength to argue with her tonight. We drive to O'Brien's and go in the back entrance. Weaver and Givits are already there, nervously fiddling around, tuning up.

"Well, hallelujah!" Weaver says as we appear.

"It's about time!" Givits says.

"We're late," Weaver says. "We were supposed to go on five minutes ago."

"Cool it guys, okay?" Sam says. He sets down his guitar and propels me out into the main room.

The room seems to come up and smash me in the face—the noise, the colors, the smoke. I haven't been out among people, except to go to the hospital, in so long. I feel dizzy, but sort of excited. People are so beautiful! It's like I'd never seen people before. The

194

way they're dressed, in their bright, crazy clothes. I feel so apart from them, like an old lady in my shawl. Sam settles me at a small table up close. In some ways I'd rather be way back, out of sight, but he wants me where he can see me. Okay.

"If you want another beer, tell them," he says. He's very nervous, I can tell.

I don't feel nervous. I know they'll be good. That's not exactly an objective judgment, I realize, but I know that once they get up there, their nervousness will go away. Still, the few moments before they get started, I watch them a little anxiously. There's so much noise. Everyone around me is talking, laughing, as though the three of them were invisible. They struggle around, getting their equipment plugged in.

"Ladies and gentlemen!" Sam yells over the voices. "Hippies, winos, whoever you are out there, may I have your attention, *por favor?* . . . Hey!"

Finally the place quiets down and they begin. It's beautiful. Sam looks at me, then away. I feel glad I came. There's pain, but the pill has removed me a little from it, as though it were some external thing. At one point, I start to cough a little from the smoke and have a minute of panic about my breathing, but it passes. Go slow, Kate. The music weaves in and out of the smoke, the pain, the people's faces, like one giant, beautiful tapestry. Sam is singing *My Sweet Lady*. He's singing to me. I feel stoned, dazzled, floating around and above the whole thing. Oh Sam, I love you.

"Tired?" Sam says. It's really late, maybe two or so. He's in high spirits. It went so well. I feel zapped, like I'd been on a roller coaster that suddenly took a deep, deep dip down and I was hanging on to the sides, hoping I wouldn't fall off.

"Wasn't it incredible?" I say. "I thought they were never going to listen . . . Then I thought they were never going to clap."

"It was great." He carries me up the walk. I put my arms around his neck. I guess I don't weigh too much now.

Sam deposits me gently on the bed. I lie back, exhausted.

"Want me to get Jill or shall we leave her down there for the night?"

In the past we would have left her because it would have meant more privacy, the chance of making love in the morning if we felt like it. "What time is it?"

"Two-thirty."

"Let's get her in the morning," I say. It seems so quiet here after all that dazzling noise, it's almost unreal.

"How did you feel?" Sam says. "Were you okay?"

I nod. "Once there was a lot of smoke and I . . . But then it was okay."

He's rummaging around in the kitchen. "Want something? Some milk?"

Sam used to make me great milk drinks when I was having cramps from my period, warm milk with a cinnamon stick and sugar. I don't feel too hungry, but I say, "Sure . . . That would be nice."

While he's heating it up, I lie back, just looking around the room. "Sam, did you move the tape recorder?"

"What?" he calls in.

"Did you put it away or something? . . . It's not here. I always keep it right next to the bed."

He comes in. "I didn't touch it." Suddenly he turns around. "The door. I always lock the door. It was open when we came back."

"Oh Jesus!"

"What else did they take, I wonder." He begins looking around. The TV is gone too and the radio.

"Remember, Mrs. What's-her-name said someone broke into her place a couple of weeks ago."

"Sam, the tape recorder! What'll I do?"

"It wasn't your fault . . . Dr. Gillman won't mind."

197

"No, but I . . . hadn't finished . . . There's still more I have to do . . . Did they take the tapes? Go check. They're in the drawer over there."

"They're still there."

"Thank God they didn't take them too."

He shakes his head. "I guess it was quite a haul for a small apartment."

"What do you think they wanted with a tape recorder?"

"They could sell it, I guess." He sits down next to me. "Kate, I'm sorry . . . Maybe Dr. Gillman can get you another or borrow another—"

"I feel she trusted me with it . . . If I hadn't gone—"

"Thank God you did! Imagine if you'd been here alone with Jill!"

"Yeah, that's right, I guess."

"We'll call her tomorrow first thing . . . I'm sure she can lend you another."

"I guess it doesn't matter much . . . I always feel like there's still so much left to say. But maybe that's always the way you feel." I sip the milk which is warm and comforting.

"Will you get a motorcycle now?" I ask, "now that we're rich?"

He grins. "Yeah, I'd like to, kind of."

"You'll be careful, though, won't you? I mean, not going too fast?"

"Sure."

I sigh and lean back.

"Do you want another pill?" Sam asks.

"Maybe I better."

We lie down together. He holds me and strokes me, what there is left of me. There's nothing to say.

Sam falls asleep and I lie awake. My chest hurts, despite the pills. I lie, watching the lights pass across the room. I feel like it, right now, like death. I get so close at night.

Death can come. Let it touch me now and I won't fight. But I dare it to come when I'm not ready. I have too much to do. My body is drugged with pain pills. I feel so warm and safe. Before I took this last one, I felt hysterical about the robbery. Something is happening to me. Am I getting close to death? I don't know. I feel afraid I am. I feel beautiful, though. Even though I haven't finished my book yet, I know I have at least touched people. Not nearly enough, though. I must work hard. I must give my whole being to Jill, Sam, and the book. I'm happy and sad, I'm human and dying; I'm a lot of things, but mostly I'm Kate, wife and lover to Sam, mother and friend to Jill, also . . .

The robbery of the tape recorder has been made into big news in the local paper. Reporters came and interviewed me for TV. It was grotesque, tiring. They propped me up in bed and asked me questions. Then, at the end they gave me a new tape recorder and a dozen reels of new tape. So I'm a celebrity. Weird. Somehow, the grotesqueness of the whole thing didn't bother me as much as I'd have expected. There's no time for all that, for fineness of feeling, for ultrasensitivity. I knew in the back of my mind that they were using me, if you want to look at it like that, but so what? It also seemed to me that people genuinely do care, that their sympathy is genuine. Maybe to them I'm like some person they've known that they never grieved for. So now they're all writing me letters, sending things. People from all over the country! A few from other parts of the world even.

What do they send? Oh, anything, everything—Bibles, letters of sympathy, miracle cures, advice. I suppose you can see all the best and worst of people in what they send, the absolute craziness and the sweetness. In the beginning, I was really touched and thought I'd try to answer all the letters. That was when I thought there'd be a dozen or so. Now, after a week, too many are coming in. Nora and Sam just leaf through them, only showing me the "best" ones. Some people send flowers. I'm not gone yet, folks! They mean well, I know.

Lying here, I can hear Nora on the phone. "Hello . . . No, this is a friend. Can I help you? . . . Well, she can't come to the phone right now, can I take a message?"

Sam forbade me to answer the phone. He's right. Save your strength. I still have my tapes to do and the important thing is to finish. He comes in, shaking his head. "Well, East Germany's got the cure today."

"What is it?"

"Some concoction mixed up in a blender—soybean oil, papaya juice and beet root."

"Ugh."

Nora comes in after him. "Well, get a load of this one," she says, reading, " 'God has a reason for everything, Mrs. Hayden, search your soul, find your sin, for you have indeed committed a terrible sin to have brought this terrible punishment on yourself and your loved—' "

Sam snatches it from her and rips it up. "Those people should be boiled in oil."

"Charity, charity!" Nora says mockingly.

"I hate those mothers," Sam says. "They're the worst . . . The religious crazies . . . The health food ones I can take."

I know what he means. They infuriate me too. What do they mean, have I ever tried Christian Science or being saved by Christ or eating a steady diet of milk and fresh spring water? Do they ever try using their heads? Why do I have this disease in the first place? Why are doctors treating me? If this is truly God's world, then we are truly God's children and are all working to make this a place we can all live in healthfully, happily, and peacefully. You don't have to go to church unless you can't do it any other way and you don't have to be saved or even pray formal prayers unless you need that crutch to get you through the day. All you need to do is get your stuff together in your head about how you feel and please don't come to me with Christ in your heart and at the same time supporting the war or spending your time in church instead of being out in the ghetto, helping God's other children in their time of need, or instead of teaching little kids Sunday school and Christ loves us, teach them that they must love one another before they can love themselves. Teach them what it is to love and cherish and to respect and to understand. Those are the things that are going to make the world a better place to live in. I don't care how many times you are saved. That doesn't make it okay to sin, just because you figure God will forgive you. Everything you do is closely examined and will reveal itself in the end. Believe me, He's there and if we don't get busy and love one another, then He's not going to love us and we are going to be in a hell of a mess.

End of sermon . . . Well, lying here all day, I tend to go off the deep end at times. But if these people really had love in them, I wouldn't mind their "sermons" to me. But so many of them seem to have these warped, hell-and-damnation minds. I know what they mean to the extent that I, more than anyone, mind the randomness of this happening, the "no reason" of it. But I prefer that to inventing reasons, especially when those reasons are that all disease is a punishment for sin. Would those people say the same thing if they'd seen those small children at the hospital, dying?

Jill trots over with a Bible and plunks it down on top of the pile. We're getting quite a collection here.

"How about lunch, Kate?"

"Oh, thanks . . . Maybe later."

Nora's been sweet. Sometimes I wish she'd go off and leave us alone, but she's really been helpful, keeping an eye on Jill and stuff. She took her to the playground a couple of times this week so Sam and I could be alone.

"I'm so glad Sam has his job, has to practice and keep regular hours. The worst would be to have him sitting around all day, holding my hand, "waiting." I don't even mind when all of them are out and I'm alone. It seems like I've gotten used to being alone, at least part of each day, and I'd miss it. I sit, the blanket around me, and talk into the tape recorder. Gypsy curls up sleepily, kind of half-listening to my voice. Sometimes I play back what I've said on other days. I'm used to the fact that my voice isn't what I think of as my voice. Now, sleepily, I flip it on and listen:

"Jill,

"I decided that before I died I wanted to write you a book. I've just begun to realize that that's exactly what I'm doing with this book.

"In it I'm trying to write of important things that happened to me, things you'll want to know later. Gee, honey, I wish I could be with you when you're old enough to read this. I wonder what you'll be like. I hope that Dad will be able to teach you all that we had planned together to teach you. By the time you read this, you'll be about fourteen or fifteen years old. I wonder what you'll be like then.

"If you ever feel the need of someone to talk to, honey, don't be afraid to come to this book. I know I can't help with all my written words, but please take comfort in knowing that whatever is wrong or whatever has made you hurt, I would have deeply cared and tried my best to understand. Perhaps that will ease the pain somewhat. I love you so much, baby. Take heart in that, please. There are so many things I always wanted to tell my daughter. Perhaps one very important thing I wanted most to say was no matter what, always do what you feel is right or best for you. Not out of selfishness, such as wanting to stay out late when you need rest for a good reason. But out of love for yourself. Treat your body and mind right and they in turn will give you health and beauty.

"If you want to sleep with a boy before you're married, please remember that sex is a function humans need to survive, but love is an emotion and through it you can be deeply hurt or given a happiness you will never forget. Don't just sleep with any man for sex. At least feel an affection, a bond of giving and receiving with him. This is so important, Jill, if you are to survive any sort of relationship. And for Pete's sake, don't get pregnant. Talk it over with your father. If you know your mind well enough, when and if this time comes, he'll feel it in the way you ask and will understand. Remember, though, he's a sensitive man. Don't hurt him."

Wow! How's that for a lecture and a bit of advice. I hope I don't sound like an old windbag. That's the trouble with this method of communication. I tend to ramble on a bit. I don't even talk that way! But I do believe it, and know that it's good and right.

Last night I had a dream that I was on an airplane and Jill was on it with Sam. She was much older, maybe a teen-ager; he looked about the same. They were talking, but I couldn't catch what they were saying. I kept leaning over, wanting to hear. Then, toward the end they came over to me. Jill looked so pretty, long, blond hair to her waist, really grown-up, lovely. She laughed and sort of nudged me and said, "You haven't done with us yet!" Almost winking like it was some kind of joke. And then they walked off.

What does it mean, I wonder. I'd like to know what will happen, what she'll be like. I lie here, thinking of her at different ages, trying to imagine, her first teacher, her first boyfriend, and then it mingles in with my own past and I don't know if I'm remembering or what.

Sam came back after the show tonight. He comes in

quietly, careful not to wake me, but I'm usually awake. I spend so much of the day in bed, half-dozing, that at night I can't sleep. Also, since the robbery I feel a little afraid, at night, of someone breaking in. I feel relieved when I hear Sam come in.

"Hi!" I call softly.

"Hi, honey."

"How did it go?"

"Pretty good . . . We tried the new song. I think it went over."

"Was the audience good?"

"Kind of . . . They can be awfully noisy . . ." He gets himself a beer. "Want one?"

"Sure."

"Was Jill okay?"

"Yeah, a little lively . . . She wanted me to read to her so I did."

"Don't let her tire you out."

"I don't . . . I like reading to her."

"How's your chest . . . Is it—"

"The same, more or less."

We talk a little tentatively. What else is there to say? We've said it all, done it all, tried our best. What we had was good and I'm glad I knew that at the time, while it was happening. I could see that looking back you would try to make it out better than it was. But I knew it was good, even the rough spots.

"Want me to play a little for you?"

"Yes." Jill never wakes up when Sam plays; he sings softly. I feel when he sings he expresses all the things he can't when he speaks. The music goes back and forth between us, like a voice, saying a lot for which there are no words.

I've run out of words. I'm getting so close to death. I look over at Jill and it hurts so bad, knowing that we will soon be losing each other. I don't even know what to say anymore. All my words of sorrow have been spent. I look at Sam. I look at his face. I think of his losing me. And of me losing him. I look at his smooth features. I can see every pore on his skin. I know every scar by heart. His smell, his breathing when he's alseep. I can almost read his mind. I'm going to miss you, honey. The way you touch me and comfort me when I'm sad. The way you love and smile. The way you dance with glee when you're happy. I'm confused, honey, not scared. What's happening to us? Where am I going? I wish in a way that I could say with some conviction that I was going to heaven. It would be so much easier. But being as human as I have become in my lifetime, I don't think I would like heaven. I don't think I would like all that gross perfection.

I can't die and leave you guys! Who's going to yell out to Jill in just the right voice to make her take a nap? Who's going to say to Sam in just the right voice, "Honey, I love you"? Who's going to clean the toilet or the oven? Who will remember when the cat needs to be wormed? What's the matter with you, God—my family's not a bunch of boy scouts who can figure out all these things for themselves. That's what you taught me to do. That's why I'm here. Why make Sam and Jill grope for answers they'll never understand the questions to? You're some kind of idiot, God, to pull something

207

like this! Especially when you know I don't care if I go to heaven or hell for saying so. What do you gain? I just don't understand.

It's funny to think that in a few more days I probably won't be here. How long can I keep breathing with these rotted lungs? It hurts now, it hurts so bad. I feel fine except for the hurt. I'd like to be up in the mountains. I hope they put me there when I die.

I'm so tired of it all. Tired of the letters and the flowers and the presents. I hope I'm not too bitter. It's hard just to go along and know you're dying. Especially now that it hurts so bad.

It's probably going to be within a week or so. A week or so . . . it's so hard to think about it being so soon. So many things I haven't done. What will happen to the book?

When I was expecting Jill, I remember how I packed my suitcase ahead of time to be ready when the time came. If I had my choice, I'd like to die at home, but I know that's not likely. It will be in the hospital. So I have some things in the suitcase, my poems and things. I'm ready.

Will that make it easier, being away from my home, from Jill, from Gypsy? Will it be like one step closer to death? I don't know. If I come back in another life I hope it will be as a cat. I would like to be here, sleeping in the sun, rubbing up against Jill's leg. I think a life as a cat would be fine. Or even as a plant. Growing in the sunlight. That wouldn't be bad, either.

"Kate, do you want your pill?"

It's Sam. I guess I half dozed off while he was playing.

Not real sleep, I could hear the music in the background.

I swallow the pill with some beer.

"You'll sleep well now," Sam says, tucking me in.

The last few nights, Jill has woken up with a bad dream. Once I slept right through it and Sam only told me about it in the morning. It's hard to tell if it's a bad dream or what. She'll wake up and come to our bed, wanting comfort. I don't like the idea of being so asleep I don't hear her. I want to be there if she wakes up again.

It's so quiet now.

"Mommy?"

It's Jill, standing near the bed. I reach over to touch her and suddenly something rises up and it's like a bag was thrown over my head. I can't breathe. I can't breathe!

Sam!

Part Three

In the pastel shades
of winter's easy way
I grasp to feel your hand
to touch, to hear, to see
and understand
why it is life
must be continued
alone
in another land.

I'm in the hospital. I won't be coming out again.
I can breathe, though. They did something to clear
my lungs. What happened last night? I can't remember.
Jill was near the bed, I started to speak and then
everything went black.

I don't feel bad now. Sleepy, far away. They must
have given me something for the pain. That's okay.

"Hey, how do you feel?"

It's Sam, trying to smile.

"Okay . . . It's great to breathe again."

"I brought my competition." He puts the tape recorder down near me.

I look at it. My beautiful machine. Did I say anything I wanted to, anything worth saying, anything that will help Jill? If I didn't, then at least I tried. I'm not up to any more.

When I open my eyes again, Sam isn't there. I can't tell if I dozed off or what. Nora is sitting there. "Sam had to go to work," she says.

"Yes, I think he said . . . I can't remember . . . Where's Jill?"

"The lady upstairs said she'd stay with her."

"I worry about her so much!"

"You shouldn't, Kate."

"But will Sam take care of her? I don't want her in an orphanage . . . How can he? He has his work. She's not really his. Why should he be saddled with her for the rest of his life? After all this crud with me. It's enough. When I die, he ought to just walk away."

"If he does, I'll take Jill. If you want me to."

"It's between you and Dr. Gillman . . . But I guess she's too busy."

"I'd raise her right, Kate."

I look at her. Her long, dark hair. That funny smile she has. Then I think of Sam's mother, the other extreme. If you could shake them both up in a bottle, you'd get one person who was just right. "If only Pat was older . . . But I don't know if she'd want a child right now . . . She's not even out of high school."

214

"What is it about me that bothers you?"

I can't help smiling. "You're messy."

"True."

"You're . . . you slept with Sam."

Her face changes. "Just a couple of times," she says. "Do you think that was such a crime under the circumstances?"

"Maybe not . . . I sound so middle-class . . . But I want Jill to have stability and order in her life . . . You've been good with her, Nora. Thanks."

"I wanted to do it."

It's funny to think that soon I won't be here. I feel fine except for the breathing. I wonder if I said the right thing to Nora. What did I say? "Nora, I—"

But she's not there anymore. I don't remember her leaving. Did I say good-bye to her? Sam is standing near the window. "Will you put the quilt and stuff in a chest? I never got around to it."

"I will."

"And the tapes—"

"I'll have them typed and bound."

"I should have arranged them. You'll never be able to tell which comes where. I'm so damn disorganized."

"No, you're not."

Dying's such a hassle."

"Don't worry about it . . . I'll sort it out."

His face is going away, just slowly. Is he leaving?

"Sam?"

"What, honey?"

"Could you call Dr. Gillman?"

"Kate . . . wait."

He begins coming back again. He looks so frightened.

"You keep fading away and coming back . . . Like some artsy-craftsy movie."

"Dr. Gillman's coming."

"About Jill—"

"I'm going to take care of Jill. What do you think I am?"

"Okay."

"I love her."

"Marry someone . . . who'll be good with her."

"Stop pawning me off on other people . . . I'm married to you."

It's odd. He can't accept it. He's frightened.

Dr. Gillman says, "What do you want for lunch, Kate?"

"A pain pill . . . But don't give me any other drugs to prolong it."

"I won't."

"I want to die on my own clock, all right?"

She nods.

Sam says, "I can't take this, I'm sorry. I—" He runs out.

I look at her. Our eyes meet. "What did I tell you? Mr. Vanishing Act."

"It's hard to watch someone die," Dr. Gillman says. "Maybe harder than it is to die."

Good-bye, Sam.

What am I thinking? Not much. About friends and places and dogs I've had. I'm thinking about my little girl, just two, kind of stubby, with golden-blond hair and an attitude toward life that makes me feel small. Thinking about dying and about me and feeling rage that soon there will be no more me. It's hard now. Very hard. I keep thinking, let me wake up just one more morning. There's so much more I have to say to Jill. It's so important.

Good-bye, Jill. Jill, my love, my little love. Hang in there, baby.

"Is Sam there?"

"He may be out in the waiting room now. I'll check."

I know he's not there. "Is my mother here?"

"No . . . Would you like me to call her?"

"Stay with me . . . I was going to be brave. But now . . . Would you hold my hand?" Dr. Gillman pulls up a chair and takes my hand.

"Is there anything you want to talk about, Kate? Anything you want me to take care of?"

She seems to be so far away, though I can hear her words. I close my eyes; it's easier. I was a virgin when I married David. All the things Mama accused me of . . . I loved keeping myself a virgin because she taught me to and I loved her and believed her. Even when she didn't believe me, I went on believing her . . . How could she accuse me of being a tramp? I hurt so bad . . . I want my mommy to comfort me. "Mama—"

"I'll tell her."

I wonder why Jill is here, why they let her come. I didn't know they allowed children. She looks so nice, playing over there. I don't think she sees me. She's building something with her blocks, some kind of house. The sun looks so pretty on her hair. I always wanted a little girl with blond hair.

On November 10, 1971, Jacquelyn Helton died. She was twenty years old.